WHAT OTHERS ARE SAYING ABOUT
A SHOPKEEPER'S MANUAL

What every retailer needs is a daily "how to" survival guide and Mary Liz Curtin has filled the bill! Great information that can be implemented immediately and you'll ask yourself "Why didn't I think of that?". Practical, references galore and fun to read—every retailer needs to add this book to their library. Thank you Mary Liz!!

Sonia Mott, Motif Home Decor

If you are a retailer, and you love your business, you have to read this book...Just when you thought there were no new ideas, along comes A Shopkeeper's Manual to shatter that myth.

Andrea Grossman, Mrs. Grossman's Paper Company

I've been in the "social expression" industry for a dozen years and I can honestly say that Mary Liz Curtin is one of the smartest people in the business. Plus, she's funny! It's a combination that allows her to deliver topical, thorough seminars and magazine articles with wit, intelligence and charm."

Betsy Cox, Brand Manager, Avanti Press, Inc.

Mary Liz's practical expertise is delivered with insight and humor. Her fresh approach offers information useful to all retailers.

Bill Winsor, president and CEO, Dallas Market Center

"I absolutely love taking classes from Mary Liz Curtin. She gives the best marketing and trade show tips; I accomplish so much more for my business with what I learned in the new buyer class she taught, and I will continue to take her classes whenever our paths cross. In fact, I will travel to a convention, just to hear Mary Liz talk. Being in a class with Mary Liz is like a sponge taking in an ocean of information she has to offer. From Marketing, to Merchandising, to eBay, Mary Liz has an entertaining, yet direct way to get her message across."

Winona Dulka
Weaving Memories (Scrapbooking and Paper Crafting)
Springfield, IL

D1279090

A SHOPKEEPER'S MANUAL

FROM THE
PENNY PINCHING RETAILER

Mary Liz Curtin

AS SEEN IN
GIFTWARE NEWS

BE A BETTER MERCHANT
RAISE YOUR MARGINS
LOWER YOUR COSTS
MAKE MORE MONEY
HAVE MORE FUN

www.wickedqueenpress.com

Cover Design by Oona Tropeano
Design & Composition by Andrew J. Pinard

Printed in the United States of America.

ISBN 0-9776243-0-7
Library of Congress Control Number: 2005910198

First Edition
9 8 7 6 5 4 3 2 1

Dedicated to my favorite retailers:

The retailer who raised me, Bert Curtin;

The retailer who gave me my first job, Judy Patterson;

The retailer who married me, Stephen Scannell;

And you, the retailer who bought this book.

Acknowledgments

This book has my name on the cover, but I certainly did not do it alone. The cover was designed by the glamorous Oona Tropeano, who is incredibly talented, takes a swell picture and is rottweiler-like in her determination to produce a beautiful product.

Penny Webster kept the project going, sourced, and edited endlessly. She also provided inspiration, often by raising her fist and shouting, "Onward!", when the project seemed stalled.

Sharla Whalen spent hours looking for typos, errors and repetition, a task that must have seemed endless but is certainly not thankless.

Andrew J. Pinard not only designed the book, but upgraded it, helped edit, refused to allow shortcuts, and never sounded aggravated, which I am sure he was. Working with him was a complete joy.

I thank all of them, but most of all I thank my loving husband, Stephen Scannell and almost perfect children, Keara and Kegan.

Contents

PART I: MERCHANDISING AND DISPLAY

PART II: MARKETING AND PROMOTION

PART III: MEETINGS, MARKETS AND MINGLING

PART IV: MONEY MATTERS

PART V: MAKING CUSTOMERS HAPPY

PART VI: MEMORABLE MERCHANTS

Foreword

I first met Mary Liz Curtin at the San Francisco International Gift Fair in 2001, and we immediately formed a friendship. Her sharp wit, knowledge, optimism, and practical approach to retailing was an immediate attraction.

She was at the fair to give a talk to gift retailers, and as I asked about her topic and she began to explain her approach to me, an idea began to form that perhaps she could share her experiences, insights, wisdom, and her wonderful sense of humor with readers of Giftware News. We later met at the California Gift Fair in Los Angeles, and the idea of her column of The Penny Pinching Retailer was born. It appeared in the December 2001 issue of Giftware News and has become one of the magazine's most popular writings. To me, Mary Liz is the Dave Barry of retail writing, but with much more substance to her columns.

Mary Liz has been "in the trenches" on several fronts in retailing. Her mother was a retailer, she and her husband operated (and again operate) a retail store, and she was a national sales manager on the wholesale side as well, all of which has added to her innate intelligence.

As Mary Liz continued to write for Giftware News and continued to criss-cross the country on speaking engagements for just about every imaginable trade meeting in just about every imaginable industry, people began to ask her where they could buy her book. She didn't have a book.

Mary Liz now has a book—and this is it. Taken from her columns in Giftware News, plus additional material, these popular writings have been reworked and formatted into not just a good read but a practical workbook for implementing many of her ideas.

I am confident that every reader will benefit from this book, and become better and more successful at retailing.

John Saxtan
Editorial Director
Talcott Publishing

Introduction

I absolutely love independent retail. I am a fan of the little box, the single store location, the small chain and the specialty retailer. I love to visit a new store not knowing what product I will see or how it will be displayed until I get inside ... and then not see another store just like it in the next town I visit.

Give me a store where they know my name (or look like they might learn it), a business that knows its customers and works to provide the product and service those customers want. Shopping is more than just buying what you need: it is leaving the store with a happy memory of a pleasant transaction. A great store makes you want to return not just for the merchandise, but because it is a nice place to be. In addition to ambience and friendship, a good store provides knowledge. Independent retailers and their employees have the how-to answers, from plumbing to setting beautiful tables.

Running an independent business of any kind has always been hard work. Small store owners have been multi-tasking since long before there was a name for it. Most of us are raising families, running the store, volunteering someplace and trying to keep ahead of the competition, which is all around us at every step. Let's face it, a person could get tired from all this.

I am married to a merchant. The Penny Pinching Retailer column began as I watched my incredibly cheap husband survive the ups and downs of the economy and actually make money in the bad times. He is an excellent shopkeeper. He buys well, watches his margins and never wastes money. The lessons I have learned from watching him were the inspiration for my column.

My husband closed his store, The Cargo Hold, at the end of 2001. Now he and I are working together in our new store, Leon & Lulu. We are proud to be a true mom and pop operation, complete with two potential second generation shopkeepers.

I hope this book will help you make more money, sell more products and run a better business. Even more, I hope it helps you have a good time while you are doing it.

Mary Liz Curtin

How to use A Shopkeeper's Manual

This manual is designed to be used as a workbook, a journal and a notebook for your ideas as well as a reference book. The chapters are loosely organized by topic, but certainly do not have to be read in the order presented. By the way, I know I mention a few things repeatedly, like the importance of re-merchandising your store frequently and looking for items with good margins. Because this book started out as a collection of columns, some things tend to reappear, especially things I consider vitally important.

Make this book yours. Have fun with it. If a chapter gives you an idea, write it down. I also encourage you to scrawl in the margins, highlight things you like and cross out anything you find disagreeable. Ask yourself these questions as you read:

+ What were the key points for your store in this chapter?
+ Give yourself credit: What do you do now that works well?
+ Did you get a new idea or inspiration?
+ You may also want to jot a few notes for a To Do Now List, as well as a To Do Later list.

If you prefer a form for the notes, we've included one at the end of the book for you to copy and use as often as you like.

But only do all that if that is what you want to do ... as I said, it's your book. Please use it, abuse it and enjoy it. If you fill it up, and need more room, call me. I'll send you a new one.

I

Merchandising and Display

1

Sense and Sensibility...

We always talk about visual merchandising. There are lots of seminars, books, and articles on the subject. Every major store has a department dedicated just to display. But why stop with the visual? What about auditory and tactile merchandising? We have five senses, and a complete retail experience should appeal to every one of them. When a customer walks into your store, you want to give her the true sense-surround experience.

Visual Merchandising is all about the eyes and gets plenty of press, so we'll just acknowledge that it is the most important of all the senses in retail, but not part of this chapter.

Tactile Merchandising is one of the many advantages stores have over Internet businesses. Most customers like to hold an item before they buy it. They love to feel the fabric and touch the texture. Once a customer has an item in her hand, the chance of her buying it is more than double. Anything you can do to get your customers to pick up the merchandise will help sell it, so make your displays accessible and appealing. Many shopkeepers put price tags on the bottom of the goods so the customers are forced to lift the items to see the prices. When you are showing products to your customers, hand the item to the shopper so she can hold it, feel it, and touch it.

Taste Merchandising really works. Just visit Costco, Whole Foods, or Trader Joe's to see sampling programs in action and watch the number of customers who buy what they try. Taste Merchandising obviously depends on your product mix, and there will be no bad taste/good taste jokes today. Almost any gift store can carry gourmet items, even if only at the holidays, and will do well with the category, especially if they have tastings. At the very least, serve your customer water or coffee as she shops. Offering customers a beverage or treat is a great way to welcome them into the store and keep them in it longer.

Auditory Merchandising sells product and sets the mood in your store. This is a sense that is easy to overlook. Many of us turn the radio to an easy-listening or light jazz station and never think about it again. Don't do it! Add music to your mix and play the CDs you sell. Vary the selections throughout the day—and always tell your customers that you are selling what they hear. If you and the staff are getting a little droopy, try a Sousa march to liven things up. Choosing appropriate background sounds for the shop will influence everyone's mood.

Who is your store?

Every shop has a personality. What's yours? Take the time to think about your shop's unique characteristics so you can build on them and develop the brand. When you describe your store for your business plan or to your staff, talk about the ambience and mood in the store as well as more prosaic issues.

Sometimes customers aren't aware of why they like a store. They just do. Talk to your customers and ask them why they like your store and what makes them come back. The answers may surprise you!

Coffee bean tip

Are your customers suffering from nasal confusion after sampling the scents in your candle or personal care areas? Provide a large salt shaker full of coffee beans for them to sniff. The coffee aroma clears the nose and makes it safe to smell again, allowing them to continue smelling and shopping.

Olfactory Merchandising is often neglected. Smells evoke memories that last a lifetime. People recall smells with 65% accuracy after a year, while the visual recall of photos sinks to about 50% after only three months. If your store smells bad, or if you have used too much fragrance, customers may just leave and some won't even know why they left.

∞

This entire chapter was inspired by a distinct and unusual aroma. My husband and I are remodeling a roller rink for our new store. (Actually, he is remodeling, and I am merely offering the occasional inspired suggestion.) If you have spent any time in a skating rink, even many years ago, you probably remember the peculiar combination of spilled soda, pizza, nacho cheese, skate lubricant, hockey-player sweat, and of course, feet.

Now, a skating rink smell isn't actually a bad smell, but it is pervasive, possibly due to a combination of the carpet near the snack bar and the 327 pairs of skates that came with the building. Visitors often say, "WOW! It smells just like it did when I was in third grade!" and they immediately become nostalgic. While the look of the establishment changed throughout the years, the smell did not.

However, it is definitely *not* a smell that will make people want to buy furniture. The distinctive odor will certainly go away when we tear the carpet out and we finish remodeling, and we will eventually have a new-store smell.

Our store will be a home store, so I want it to smell gracious and inviting. We'll carry scented candles, soaps, and home care products—all of which will give a light scent to the store. We'll serve fragrant coffee and distribute flowers and plants to keep the air fresh.

And finally, don't forget to merchandise to the sixth, and most important sense: the *Sense of Humor*. I firmly believe that when your customers laugh, their lips open, then their purses open, and they start to spend. Of all the senses, this is the easiest to lose after a hard day in retail.

By the way, I am keeping the skates. They really don't smell all that bad. My husband does not agree.

2
Who Wants Free Fixtures?

What's holding the merchandise in your store? Have you taken a good look lately? Take a little time to evaluate what you have, and think carefully about what you need and what you should stop using, update, or throw out.

Take a very close look at the display units you have received from your vendors. Don't turn your store into a forest of wire spinners.

Ask these questions: Do your fixtures hold the merchandise well? Do they add to the ambiance in your store? Do they look good together?

Regardless of the style of your store, the price points you carry, or the merchandise you select, your store should look interesting, unique, and special. You can accomplish this on a budget with a little planning, some imagination, and a strong determination to keep the look in your store consistent.

Don't put any merchandiser in your store that doesn't look right with the rest of the fixtures, regardless of price. Many companies have designed excellent units that maximize sales per square foot, show the product to their best advantage, and will look appropriate in any store. Others are not worth the money, even if you pay only the shipping. Too many mismatching displays from different companies will leave your store looking like a jumble.

TWO BASIC LOOKS

There are two basic kinds of manufacturer's displays:

1. Stock spinners or wire displays from display houses with custom header cards added are readily available and inexpensive for the company to offer.

These all look pretty much alike, with slightly different bases, colors, or types of wire. The products they hold can be changed if you change vendors, and they can be useful for a long time. They are basic and certainly serve a purpose, but are generally not breathtakingly fabulous on their own.

2. Custom fixtures are usually more expensive. Manufacturers invest a great deal of time and money to develop merchandisers that will show off their line to its very best advantage, promote the name of the company, and increase sales. These usually have a very definite style that may look perfect in your store … or not work at all.

By the way, manufacturers generally don't make any money on their merchandisers. They offer them at, near, or even below cost to increase sales of their

Keep Fixtures Full

When inventory is low, people often stop shopping. Don't let your store look picked-over or empty.

When a display is more than half empty (or half full, depending on your point of view), it is time to re-merchandise.

If inventory starts to look low, many customers think that the good stuff is gone and only the dregs are left. Always keep shelves full and faced. On slot wall or peg board, don't use long hooks unless you can fill them. If you have manufacturer's displays and the product has sold through, consider taking the fixture off the floor and putting the merchandise in something else until the reorders arrive.

Hired Hands

If you are pressed for time or inspiration think about employing a professional visual merchandiser to help with your displays. There are lots of talented people available on a part-time or consulting basis and even just a few hours a week can make a huge difference in the look of your store. This is not an easy hire, as you must find a person who shares your design ethic. A great display person is one of the most important members of a retail team and worth finding. If, like most of us, you do your own visuals, schedule the time to work on display so you will make it a priority and give it the attention it deserves.

product. It's really not very nice to buy a line just to get the fixtures to use for someone else's product.

A very few lines absolutely require their own fixtures. Often the product will not sell well without the benefits of the unit, so do plan to buy these displays if you carry the line. Only purchase units that will increase your sales of the product they hold.

Before you agree to use any manufacturer's merchandising unit, think about how it will look in your store. Is the scale correct? Will the colors work? Is the signage overpowering?

Then consider the cost. Even free fixtures will cost you the freight to bring them to the store. This can be pricey if the units are large or bulky, especially since many are shipped from a different location than the product they will display. Always get the full information about the shipping costs. Another hint: verify that the merchandise and the fixture will arrive at the same time.

Offset fixtures are not free, but the manufacturer contributes to the cost of the unit by giving you merchandise. This means that you pay up front for the fixture, and the company gives you enough merchandise to reimburse you that cost, based on the retail value of the product. While the gross profit is enough to pay for the fixture, your expenses are not taken into account, so the cost is not completely defrayed by the offset. It is still, however, usually a good deal.

Consider the merchandise you are buying. Do you plan to carry it long enough to justify the purchase of a fixture? That fixture will cut into your margins, especially if you don't have the line for long.

Also beware of using too many vendor signs. Your goal is to establish your store name, not that of the manufacturer. The only reason to promote the manufacturer's name is if your customers truly know the brand and are searching for it, or if the sign explains the product well.

Once you have a fixture, whether it came from a manufacturer, a display company, was recycled from your house or the trash (my favorite place to find furniture and fixtures), remember that it belongs to you. You can remove the sign, paint it, or reuse it any way you like as your needs change. Think about new ways to use old pieces: it is almost impossible to change your displays too often.

Here is an important rule when shopping at shows, whether you are offered a fixture or not: never, never, never, never ever buy anything unless you have a plan for its display. Of course, this is a rule that any first-class buyer breaks regularly, but it is good to start with pure intentions.

There are lots of great deals available for displays. Choose carefully and make your store memorable.

3
Spend a Little, Sell a Lot

Keeping your store looking good is a big job, but one that definitely pays off at the register. Visual merchandising (or plain old display) makes every-day products look special, helps expensive merchandise look extraordinary, and keeps your store looking fresh. In addition to the fixtures you use in your store day in and day out, props make a world of difference in the appearance and atmosphere of your store. How does a budget conscious retailer find merchandising magic? Where are the Penny Pincher's Props?

First, foremost, red flags, and the very most important tip: look for display stuff all the time. If you just keep your eyes open for interesting things that cross your daily path, you will be amazed at what you can find. Look in the trash, dig around in the mark-down bins at the big stores after each holiday, visit garage sales and flea markets.

FLOWERS, FRUIT, AND OTHER FAUNA

Recently at the Seattle Gift Show I found some terrific branches an exhibitor had discarded as she set up her booth. They were free and perfect for the wreaths and baskets we were making in a class.

Look in your garden and down the street. Are there pine cones? Sticks? A few big branches? Use them *au naturel* for a while, then paint them any color you need to pep up a display. Fresh flowers are always bright, pretty, uplifting, and give a luxurious feeling to the store, whether they come from your garden or the florist. Here's a little way to cheat: fill in your fresh arrangements with artificial flowers. You'll often pass them all off as real. (Please don't tell the Society of American Florists that I've suggested this or they'll quit hiring me!)

Permanent florals are excellent for in-store use, also. A good collection of silks is a display lifesaver and will last for years. Remember to keep them dust free.

Visit the produce department for longer lasting display props. Buy oranges, lemons, and apples to fill vases and bowls. Some vegetables, like artichokes, will dry well and be useable for years.

CHECK THE CURB

We pick trash in my family. My husband rides his bike three mornings a week on three different garbage routes, my kids often come home dragging junk from

Traditions

Do you have a great display piece that has been on the floor for a long time? Hide it for a while and then bring it back. Some customers will feel they are seeing an old friend again and others will think it is brand new.

Many stores use the same Christmas decorations over and over, especially mechanical pieces or foliage. Their customers look forward to seeing them each year, and may be upset if their favorite dancing snowmen don't appear. At my mother's store, many years ago, we had a mechanical doll who appeared in our window, trimming the tree, year after year after year. Customers loved her—they would come every year with their kids and visit her. Although we were much less smitten with her after a few years (actually, we were really sick of her) we kept her because of her relationships with the holiday shoppers.

the curb, and I have often pulled over to seize a prize from the side of the road. A fresh coat of paint on a dilapidated piece of furniture can give it new life in your store. If you are using furniture for display, you can accept imperfection gracefully. Drawers can be stuck shut (or open), doors can be missing ... as long as the piece will hold the merchandise and look interesting, it will work. Don't forget that one retailer's trash is a customer's treasure: put price tags on the pieces you have rehabilitated!

We have a fabulous collection of tables, dressers, rocking chairs and more, all of which only needed a quick paint job to turn them into shabby chic accessories.

BORROW IT

If you don't have the props you need, look to the other merchants in your area. Often you can borrow a piece of furniture, artwork, or gimcrack to use in your display in exchange for giving the other store credit. Are you doing a wedding window? Maybe you can borrow a dress. You won't know until you ask.

Price it. Sell it.

Everything in your store should be for sale, including the fixtures and props. If you are using something you don't want to part with, price it very high and you will feel better if it sells. We probably could have sold that doll in the window ...

BUY IT

Sometimes you have to break down and buy items for display. When you place orders with your regular vendors, consider adding a few bigger, more expensive pieces to make the entire collection look important. There are two kinds: the permanent things that stay in the store forever and help make it special (think of the talking tree and the clock tower at FAO Schwartz) and temporary props that help develop a theme or call attention to a group of products. These latter display pieces have a limited life span in your store and need to change frequently to keep the shop interesting. Always price the props! If you sell them, there's something else somewhere waiting for you.

When FAO Schwartz closed in Seattle, the liquidators sold most of the big, custom fixtures on eBay, including the 15-foot, two-ton bronze bear that was in front of the store. I happened to be downtown at 6:30 on a Sunday morning when the bear was being moved to a flatbed truck for the ride to his new home in front of a daycare on Bainbridge Island and met Doug Hartley, the man who bought the bear.

Doug is thrilled with his purchase. The bear was $70,000 when it was made ten years ago, and the replacement value is estimated at three times that. Doug paid only $11,800, plus tax, for a total of $12,838.40. However, as with many display items, the freight is a killer. Doug said he expects to spend another $8,000 to move the bear and repair the sidewalk.

HOW TO GET RID OF PROPS

When the time has come for a display piece to go, the best solution is to sell it. Ideally, someone will buy it at full retail; but if you have to mark it down to move it, that's OK. The short margin is more than offset by the use as a conversation piece and display.

If you cannot sell your prop at the store, try selling it on eBay. While Doug got a great bargain on his bear, many stores find eBay an excellent avenue for selling overstocks, odds and ends, and display pieces at very profitable prices.

If you have an interesting large piece, consider donating to a charity for an auction. You will help them, get a deduction, and gain publicity for your store.

One more note: don't be in a hurry to get rid of your display items. Reuse and recycle! As you dress up your store, think big. Buy something large and eye catching. Dare to make a mistake—it's only display.

HANDY DISPLAY SOURCES

Oilcloth International

Chalkcloth is black oilcloth that is fabulous for tablecloths and upholstery. You can write on it over and over and wipe it off like a blackboard. This miracle fabric is lots of fun for display and will sell well by the yard. $11.00 a yard retail. www.oilcloth.com

Blackboard Paint

Rust-Oleum Corp. makes chalk board paint in green and traditional black. It works on any paintable surface and is a great cheap wall treatment in your store. Visit www.rustoleum.com for information and www.paintideas.com for inspiration.

Behind the Glass

Do you wish you could remember the great displays you see at market? Dallas Market Center has made it easy. They offer over 70 displays from five different categories. Dallas has absolutely gorgeous showrooms with excellent displays. Log on to www.dallasmarketcenter.com for more information.

4
Ready! Set! Display!

Are you ready to make some display magic in your store? Having a well-planned toolbox ready to go when new merchandise arrives, or the window needs to be redone, will make the project faster and easier.

To begin, let me state that this is display we are talking about, not actual construction. You are making a temporary exhibit, and you will soon change whatever you create. Do not mar the surface of the walls any more than necessary, or you will either have to patch and repaint or try to make your next display cover the holes from the last few installations. While you want the merchandise to be secure, use the smallest nails or screws and the minimum amount of glue for the job.

TOOLBOX ESSENTIALS

DRILL: I find that drilling screws is faster and easier than pounding nails for pictures and wall hangings. Admittedly, it is also more fun. Look for a lightweight cordless drill (9.6 volt should be adequate) and buy a spare battery if you do a lot of work with it.

MONOFILAMENT: You'll need two weights of fishing line—a fine one to hang things invisibly and a stronger weight for heavy items. Remember that fishing line is cheap. If it gets horribly tangled, just throw it out.

GLUE GUN: I use this more for repairs than d isplay, but it is a handy addition to your tool arsenal. Often a quick fix makes an item saleable and is easier than contacting the manufacturer. If you have a hot glue gun, beware! Molten glue inflicts terrible burns. Consider a cool melt gun ... And the cordless versions are terrific.

STAPLE GUN: My favorite is the Swingline JT-21 which is lightweight and easy on the hand. Never nail when you can staple, I say. Keep a staple remover handy, too, to save your nails.

CLEANING SUPPLIES: Keep paper towels, glass cleaner, and a few rags in the toolbox so you won't be tempted to put dirty merchandise in the display.

SCISSORS: One pair of strong, sharp scissors is essential. Have a pair dedicated to the toolbox so you don't have to hunt for them. Tie a bright polka dot

---

Better sales through signage

Use signs throughout the store to describe the product as well as show the prices. This is a great way tell your customer the features and benefits of the merchandise or even a little of the story behind the product. For the perfect example, visit Restoration Hardware.

Continuity is important, so use the same typeface, style of frame and color for all signs. Make the font large enough for a person in her middle years to read without glasses and use no more than three sizes of frames.

Signs are your silent, unpaid salesperson. The one who always shows up.

ribbon to the handle to make the scissors easy to spot among the other impedimenta.

IRON OR STEAMER: Wrinkled stuff does not sell! If you carry any textiles or use fabric in your displays, press it before displaying. A professional garment steamer is worth the investment. It is quick and convenient.

TAPE MEASURE, PENCIL, & LEVEL: Hang things straight! If you are doing a presentation on a wall, plan it before you start hanging things, and measure for exact placement. Your toolbox should contain a 9" torpedo level and a retractable steel tape measure. When measuring for placement, use the ceiling or floor as a reference point.

HAMMER AND ASSORTED NAILS: In addition to the basic hammer and nails, consider including cup hooks, push pins, and tacks. Don't bother with a nail when a push pin will do. Not only will this make the task easier, your walls will suffer less damage.

PLIERS: Useful for removing nails and tacks. Hint! Always grab the end of a fastener with pliers and pull straight out forcefully. If you roll pliers against the wall it will increase leverage, but it may dent the surface.

BLACK FELT TIP MARKER: Use this for quick touch-ups and making signs fast.

REUSABLE ADHESIVE: A reusable, repositionable adhesive will straighten pictures, hang posters, and keep fragile items securely on shelves (excellent for earthquake zones) without marring the item or the surface on which it rests. It will hold items up to six ounces in weight and is just all-around handy to have. There are several manufacturers; check at your local craft store.

TOOL APRON: This is incredibly handy—put all the things you'll need in the pockets before you climb a ladder or crawl into the window. You will save trips and endless frustration if you have your tools with you.
Having these essentials (well, except for the painting stuff) ready to go when you are makes display faster. Re-merchandising your store frequently makes your inventory look new and exciting. It is also easier to dust while you are rearranging everything, and a clean store is imperative. Dusty products don't sell!

Don't be afraid of display. You can make a mistake and it just doesn't matter ... you are going to redo it anyway. Keep your store constantly changing and fun to visit. Your customers will notice and so will your bottom line. Think out of the toolbox.

Thanks, Honey

My loving husband, who can fix, hang or remodel absolutely anything, provided technical assistance for this column. He does all installation and repair the right way, which is safe, long lasting and secure. I tend to install or hang items the display way, which is quick and easy, uses the materials and tools at hand and makes the smallest holes, although my installations are sometimes a little shaky. I say there is room for both methods.

Free Display Handbook

George Little Management has a lovely gift for you: The GLM Retailer Display Tips Handbook. This book is full of ideas, resources and information on display, lighting, store layout and more. They have two versions; one for exhibitors and one for retailers. Check out the websites listed on page 154. You'll be glad you did!

5

Phenomenal, Fabulous Fome-Cor

Penny pinching retailers are always wary of spending money, but there is no better place to drop a little cash than on display, and Fome-Cor is a good use of your money. Fome-Cor is a miracle material. It is lightweight, reasonably priced, easy to use (once you have developed a few skills), and incredibly versatile. You can build almost anything with Fome-Cor, from simple sandwich signs and pedestals to intricate models. It is amazingly strong, too.

Fome-Cor, an International Paper product, is made of paper laminated to a foam interior. It comes in four by eight foot sheets, in thicknesses from $\frac{1}{8}$" to 1." There are numerous colors from which to choose, but for most display purposes $\frac{1}{4}$" white Fome-Cor is excellent. You can purchase it at most art supply stores and display houses. Always check around for the best price you'll find a wide range of retails. For the best value, buy a full case of 25. I always buy white Fome-Cor and paint it if I need another color. It is also helpful to have the case box to store the unused sheets, keeping them clean and undamaged. You may also consider sharing a full case with another merchant.

What will you do with this miracle material? Make pedestals large enough to hold a cardboard dump of product or small enough to use inside a jewelry display case. Cut a piece of Fome-Cor into a shape, paint a sign on it and suspend it from the ceiling. Construct a backdrop for your window or a special display. Make big paper dolls to dance along the back of your cash wrap ... once you start playing with it you'll find lots of uses.

There are many similar materials on the market, from poster board and Homasote to Gator Board and Sintra. Each is perfect for a specific use, but I think the most versatile and easy to use for general display is Fome-Cor.

Fome-Cor fanatic

Even after building many booths with Fome-Cor, some more successful than others, I regard this material with awe and wonder. It is a material that will help you build a fixture in a pinch, construct a wall right where you need one. You can cover it with fabric, paint it (if you are very careful), cut it, pin it and even reuse it.

BEFORE YOU START

CLEAN HANDS: Don't forget that the exterior of Fome-Cor is only paper, and paper's biggest enemies are water and dirt. Wash your hands and dry them well before beginning construction. One more tip: the Fome-Cor's shipping case is usually dusty, so wash twice.

BEWARE DENTS AND DINGS

Careful! The corners are fragile and dent easily. Don't bang them around. Also, this material dents easily, so don't kneel or lean on it while you are cutting.

EQUIPMENT

SHARP KNIFE: the key to a clean cut is a really, really sharp blade. While some display people use box knives, I prefer a matte knife. Bruce Baker, Fome-Cor artist extraordinaire, swears that a scalpel is the only instrument sharp enough for the task. Whatever you choose, change the blades often and treat the tools with respect—these knives are dangerous! It is absolutely impossible to remove blood from Fome-Cor, so be careful.

PINS: long straight pins with round heads or long T-pins are excellent for attaching the pieces of your masterpiece. Using pins also allows you to dismantle the piece for storage and later use.

TAPE: clear or white 2" tape can be used for construction. When using tape, be sure your tape application is even and straight so there are no wobbly lines. Never try to remove the tape as it will almost always tear the paper. If you need to re-tape, cut the tape and start over.

STRAIGHT EDGE: a four-foot ruler or drywall T-square is essential for straight cuts. If you are in a pinch you can use another piece of Fome-Cor, but it is not as efficient.

TECHNIQUES

PAINTING: Fome-Cor can be painted, but do it gingerly. You can roll or brush paint on it, but spray paint is the easiest for a light coat. Don't use too much or it will soak into the material and weaken the board. If the color is not dark enough, use several light coats.

WORKSPACE: These sheets are big, so you may not have a counter large enough to set the material on to work with it. I usually cut Fome-Cor on a drop cloth on the floor.

SCORING & CUTTING: Using your straight edge, make your first cut through the paper only. Stand the board with the scored side away from you and gently pull the two sides toward you. This will break the foam evenly. Then cut the back side of the paper and you will have a perfect, clean edge.

You can also score the board and fold it without cutting all the way through (scored side out) to make the base for a pedestal or table. With this method, you only have to close one side. This will work for a variety of shapes, from a triangle to an octagon.

Move It!

You cannot change your displays too often. Every time you move the product around, re-merchandise a display or rearrange your fixtures, the store appears new and different. Plan on a total reset of the store at least for times a year and schedule new product to arrive at the same time. The combination of the fresh display and the new merchandise will make older product look new and give the employees, as well as the customers, a lift. An added benefit to moving product is that you will be forced to dust.

PINNING: Use two-inch display pins to close your pedestal. Just push them through both layers until they are flush. As you are closing the table, be certain that it is even and square. Fome-Cor is very strong if perfectly vertical, but if your table is skewed it will lose its structural integrity.

TAPING: If you are doing a large backdrop and have to join pieces of Fome-Cor, your seams will be prettiest if you tape from the back. Working on a clean floor, you may need a friend to help pull the tape from one end to the other. Don't step on the Fome-Cor!

COVERING: Use fabric to cover Fome-Cor for use as a backdrop or platform. Use pins to attach the fabric to the board and be sure to cut away the excess fabric from the corners so you have a flat, mitered corner. Use covered boards as back drops or platforms for products.

REUSE! RECYCLE!

Always keep your used Fome-Cor. If one side is dirty, turn it over. When both sides are distressed, paint it or cover it. Stack soiled pieces beneath clean ones if you need additional thicknesses for strength or height.

Fome-Cor is an inexpensive and easy way to build displays and temporary fixtures that will help you keep your store looking exciting and new. And always think like a surgeon: use a sharp knife and clean hands.

USEFUL DISPLAY WEBSITE

There is a website devoted to visual merchandising, mannequins, and display. Visit www.fashionwindows.com for inspiration, resources, ideas, tips, and techniques, including detailed instructions for building a pedestal out of Fome-Cor.

They also have some great ideas for seasonal store windows. I found some excellent free information here. If you want all their services and access to the full graphics, there is a $4.95 monthly fee, which is a bargain if you are at all serious about display.

6

The Power of Paint

Nowhere can you get so much impact for such little money as with a can of paint. Many storeowners are afraid of paint, but as with most display techniques, the trick is not to take it too seriously. You don't have to repaint the entire store. Try a bright seasonal color on the wall behind your cash wrap or in the window. Repaint your endcaps, a few fixtures, or the back door.

How does the back wall of your store look? Consider a vibrant tone to bring your customers all the way through the shop. If you paint a frequently touched area like a back door, I recommend satin or semi-gloss paint. For other less frequently touched areas, flat paint will be fine. Note: flat paint hides imperfections in the under surface better than satin or semi-gloss. Always use latex paint for its ease of clean up.

A quick update of a few colors will give your entire store a lift, make the merchandise look new, and even revitalize your staff.

Life is a great big canvas,
and you should throw all
the paint on it you can.

—Danny Kaye
U.S. actor & singer
(1913–1987)

START WITH THE WALLS

Take a good look at your store. Where are the walls looking worn, dirty, or just plain tired? Will you have to paint everything or can you just highlight one area? If the entire store needs refreshing, you will have to decide how to attack the project. Ideally, try to do the job in parts so that you don't have to close the store while you work. A plan will make the task less daunting.

As you plot each section of the store, think about the merchandise you will show there, how you will display it, and what fixtures you will use. Your store does not have to be all one color, of course, but the hues you use must work well together so that the shop does not turn into visual chaos.

You'll need the proper equipment. The basics are a roller frame, roller covers, roller pan, one inch, one and one half inch, and two inch brushes, an edging tool, a drop cloth, masking tape, and rags. Also keep a roll of plastic wrap in the bucket to wrap wet brushes and rollers between coats. Use a sturdy ladder—it is hard to paint well when you are in danger of falling. Store your painting gear (except the ladder) together in a box or bucket so that it is ready go when you are. You'll need a roller frame, roller covers, roller pan, one inch, one and one half inch, and two inch brushes, an edging tool, a drop cloth, and rags.

Before you start to paint, clear the area and put down a drop cloth so you have room to work and move your equipment around easily. I also suggest you wear an apron, although old clothes are even better. This is advice I give but rarely remember to heed, so I have lots of paint-spattered clothing. Keep a damp rag handy to mop any drips as soon as they drop.

WEED YOUR FIXTURES

Are they a little dingy? Do you have a thousand wire racks that you got because they were free? Mismatched or worn cabinets, units that are chipped or scuffed? Throw out the ugly or unused ones! Yes, get rid of them. Crummy fixtures make the products they hold look bad and empty units make the store look under-stocked.

Occasionally, empty each fixture, clean it well and look at it carefully. Touch up little marks and dings or repaint it before you replace the goods. Sometimes just a good cleaning and re-merchandising is all a fixture needs.

IS IT TRASH OR TREASURE?

There are lots of free display units available to you every week, just needing a little care and perhaps a coat of paint. Yes, there they are at the curb, waiting for you to take them home or to the store. Some of the greatest display units I've seen have been picked from the trash. As you are shopping garage sales and picking up roadside recyclables, remember that for display you have different standards than for home use. Drawers and doors can stick a little or even be missing if the piece is good looking.

After reading several books on furniture painting and worrying about doing it correctly, I have developed this somewhat casual (approaching lazy) method that has worked very well. Place the object on newspapers or a drop cloth. First, wash all surfaces you plan to paint. Sand lightly (I just can't face stripping paint) and wipe off the dust. I choose a base color and paint the whole thing. I have a basket filled with small bottles of latex paint in lots of colors, so I have an array of possibilities to choose from. I mix another color with Behr's Faux Glaze (no proportions, put some glaze in a cup or bowl and squirt some paint in, then mix. A small amount of paint goes a long way) and do a coat over the first. The glaze allows the first color to show through and gives an interesting effect. You can put many layers of different colors and just keep experimenting until you like the result. Experiment with rubbing the paint off with a rag or sponge if it is too dark.

You can paint parts of the piece different colors. The bright blue painter's tape is worth the extra money for masking. Be sure the previous coat of paint is dry before you put it down. Finish the project with two or three coats of satin finish water base polyurethane to protect the surface.

Faux Finishing

I have a porch filled with furniture in various stages of completion. When I re-paint furniture purchased at garage sales, found at the curb or rescued from a basement, I am amazed at the changes I can make quickly and with little effort. There are lots of great books on the subject, but I have one very important tip: don't take it too seriously. You can always change it.

Think of paint as make-up for the store. You can try new colors, have a little fun, and give the shop a lift. Just as a new lipstick gives your face a new look, a bright color on a wall or two will make a big difference to the entire space. Your shop will look fresh, the merchandise will show better, the change will help energize your employees, and most important, customers love the excitement of a new color.

Be daring! Go out on a limb!

You can always repaint.

7
Housekeeping for Shopkeepers

When a person thinks of opening a store, housekeeping is just not one of the activities he or she envisions. Maybe you imagine happily using a beautiful feather duster or running the vacuum for a minute just before you open the doors and the hordes rush in, but the truth is far grittier. Everything gets dirty, dusty, and grimy, stores included. They are dusty places made even dustier by frequently opening doors, arriving freight, and peripatetic people.

People don't like to buy dirty merchandise. They won't even pick products up if the dirt is visible. Naturally, the longer the goods are on the shelf, the dustier they get, which lessens their chance of being sold. Also, the slower the product moves, the less you like it, which makes it harder to get motivated to clean it.

Shops have to be maintained to a standard that appears high (certainly higher than the standards in my house). Your store doesn't actually have to be all that clean, but it has to look clean. Fortunately, you probably don't cook much in the store, so at least you don't have to deal with grease, unless you are located close to a restaurant.

When was the last time you gave your store a thorough cleaning? Take a walk outside, come back in, and think about what needs to be done.

WINDOWS

Your store windows have to sparkle. While you can certainly hire a service to clean them, that is expensive. Window washing is not difficult if you have the right equipment. A janitorial supply store can provide you with an extendable pole that will easily reach the very top of your tallest window. You need two attachments: a 10" or 14" T-shape strip washer, which has a removable cleaning pad, and a T-shaped squeegee. Get a bucket large enough for the strip washer to fit in easily, and a few rags to wipe the squeegee, and you are set. Plain hot water is adequate for most windows, and a little white vinegar really makes them shine. Don't forget to change the water when it gets dirty or you will just spread the dirt around. Check your windows when the sun is the strongest to see if it is time to wash them.

Need I mention that the worst thing in a window is dead flies? Don't let your window become their final resting place. Check frequently in the summer for the recently departed.

OUTSIDE

Check the area outside your store for garbage, cigarette butts, or worse left by

Dirt alert

My household includes my loving husband, 2 untidy children, three cats and a rottweiler named Lulu in a house perpetually under construction, so I know far more than I'd like about disorder and dirt. Since I travel frequently and all of them are completely oblivious, I have had to lower my standards and discovered that the place doesn't really have to be perfect. They have taught me that a little dust won't kill you and that no matter how much the dog hair piles up it never resembles carpet.

For the home, the best motivator for cleaning is to invite a houseguest or have a party. In the store, I find that frequent re-merchandising keeps the shelves clean, but we still have to dust mop or vacuum the floors every day.

passersby or their dogs. Sweep or hose as needed. If you have plants, keep them healthy. Be sure the front door is clean and the handle is not sticky.

FLOORS

Spend the big money on a good vacuum! Get one that is light and easy to use so you and the staff don't have to wrestle with it. Don't be seduced by attachments. You really only want power and ease of use. If you have uncarpeted floors, a tank vacuum easily reaches the back corners where the balls of dirt congregate. Dust mop the floors frequently. Wet mop with hot water when the dirt starts to show and use cleaning supplies only for stubborn or greasy dirt, as they can cause build-up that will dull the shine on the floors.

SHELVES

I believe that if you are going to clean your shelves, you may as well rearrange them. That will give you the maximum satisfaction and help keep your store looking interesting. Don't worry about the chaos you may create in the store when you take everything off the shelves as you work. It makes the store look exciting and customers are always intrigued by the activity. Dust the products as you remove them from the shelves, clean the shelves, then create a new display. A feather duster is great for a daily tidying.

GLASS

This is the hardest part of storekeeping and requires relentless vigilance. Eradicate fingerprints on display cases and the front door daily. All glass merchandise must be clean to sell. Remember the maintenance factor when you are buying glass display units.

A FEW OTHER THINGS TO CLEAN IN YOUR SPARE TIME

Come in early one morning, get on the ladder, and clean your track lighting before the bulbs get hot. You will be amazed at the difference in the light which clean bulbs give. (This hint is from my mother, Bert Curtin, who suggests it for your house as well.)

Dust the tops of all displays and fixtures. Remove clothing from displays and dust the rods it hangs on.

Help the Clutter Blind

After a long trip, coming home to a tidy house means a lot to me. It doesn't really have to be all that clean, as long as the junk is picked up and it appears orderly. In an unusual moment of parental frustration, just off the plane, I was hollering at my family about the junk that was everywhere. My son, Kegan, was about 13. He put his arm around me, sighed deeply and said "The problem is, Mom, we are clutter blind. We just don't see it". I had to laugh at that and agree to spare their lives.

Are you and your staff clutter-blind? The cash wrap and receiving counters tend to be the places where this terrible affliction has its biggest impact. While we are still seeking a cure, be sure to treat the symptoms and pick up the extraneous stuff.

If you are feeling really ambitious, pull the cash wrap apart and clean behind your bags and supplies. Wipe down your cash register and use compressed air to blow the dirt out from the keys and the back of the drawer. Clean the phone, especially the mouthpiece.

BUY GOOD EQUIPMENT

While I always advocate saving money, good equipment is worth the price. First-rate tools work better, last longer, and are easier to use. Save money on labor by doing chores yourself, but always buy quality appliances and equipment.

DON'T TAKE IT TOO SERIOUSLY

While you may decide to do a major cleaning of every single thing in your store once in a very great while, remember that the trick is to keep the shop *appearing* clean. They say that cleanliness is next to godliness. If you watch out for fingerprints and take care of the visible dust, you are halfway to heaven.

8

Check Out Your Cash Wrap

The kitchen is the heart of the home. By the same logic, the cash wrap is the core of the store, the soul of the shop, the epicenter of the emporium. It's where we spend the most time and the part of the store that makes the last impression on a customer. It is probably not an overstatement to say the cash wrap is the most important spot in your store.

This is where the staff tends to congregate, where a shopper has a few minutes to wait while her purchase is completed, where the business of the store is conducted. It's often where we work with reps, answer the phone, write orders, and check in freight. It is also where shoppers have a chance to add a few little things to their purchases and where you have a few minutes to chat with the people as they check out.

Unfortunately, just like the kitchen counter, the cash wrap's counter is often home to projects in the works, piles of merchandise, stray tools, coffee cups, lists, messages, notes, and or detritus of all kinds. You may find damaged goods waiting to be returned to the vendor, inventory waiting to be re-stocked, things to be fixed, and gifts waiting to be wrapped. Everything happens here, and sometimes it looks as if it all happened at once, like a natural disaster. Without constant attention, it is easy for this important area to resemble the junk drawer even more than the kitchen counter.

This is not the way to treat the most valuable real estate in your store. Here's my six step plan for a more profitable check out counter.

Cash Drawer Drama

Teach your cashiers to break coin rolls on the edge of counter rather than banging them against the open drawer, which can severely damage the drawer mechanism.

Also, remind cashiers to think ahead and keep sufficient cash in the drawer for change. Customers hate to wait while the staff scrambles to find money to complete a transaction.

STEP ONE: ORGANIZE IT

First, get rid of the big stuff. Clear the work surfaces, get rid of the junk, and put away everything you can. Assign convenient spots for the tools you use regularly, and put your other apparatus where nobody can see it. Arrange your packaging and gift wrapping supplies neatly, and throw out anything you don't use regularly. See if some things can be moved to the back room, like packages waiting to be shipped or broken items you are planning to repair.

Having the cashier's area well organized will help speed up your transactions and make your staff more efficient, which will give customers a good impression as they leave the store. As an added bonus, if your staff is able to package and wrap purchases easily, without searching for things, they will be able to concentrate on interacting with the customers.

STEP TWO: CLEAN IT

Get serious with dirt. Clean all surfaces, vacuum the dust from the backs of shelves and the corners of drawers. Continue to get rid of the stuff you don't need everyday while you are cleaning. Wipe off all fingerprints and spots, wash the wastebasket. Clean the keys on the register, and wash the phone. Remove the sticky stuff from the scissor blades, pitch the pens that do not work, and dispose of everything extraneous.

STEP THREE: ANALYZE IT

High priced real estate

The front counter is some of the very best real estate in the store as customers often buy the things they find there while they wait. Keep this assortment of merchandise interesting and changing so the regulars find new things each time they make a purchase.

Check the front of the desk often—customers often drop papers, candy wrappers and other junk there. Think of this as the Rodeo Drive of your store and keep it glamorous at all times.

Now that you have cleared the decks, go around to the front of the desk and pretend you are a customer. What do you see? Every single thing your customer sees should look tidy, clean, and appealing. This is the area in the store where people linger the longest, so make it memorable.

Shoppers should be comfortable: Are there places to write a check and to set a purse?

If it takes a while to make a sale or write up customer orders, consider a stool or chair so your customers are comfortable while they wait.

STEP FOUR: SIGN IT

Your signage should be clear and simple and coordinate with the décor of your store. First, tell your customers what you do for them. Do you gift wrap? Is shipping available? Remind them about your gift registry and mailing list. Add your web address to the sign, too.

State your store policies clearly and *positively*. Something like, "Returns cheerfully accepted within 14 days, with receipt," rather than the more direct, "No returns after 14 days no matter what. Don't even think about trying to bring anything back after two weeks, and if it is in an opened box we won't even look at it ever." If you were the customer, which would you prefer to hear? Keep all policies friendly.

STEP FIVE: MERCHANDISE IT

Everybody knows that the check out counter is the best sales area in the store. It is a great place to show jewelry, small pickup items, seasonal treats, and greeting cards. Plan the product offering carefully to maximize your add-on sales. Show a variety of price points—it is amazing how many things people will buy (and how much they will spend) at the very end of the shopping experience. Customers often seem to feel that if they're in for a nickel, they're in for a dime. So pay special attention to this area and buy product for it. Don't just put the leftovers and odds and ends at the register.

STEP SIX: STAFF IT

Everybody has to help keep this essential area looking great. Ask your staff to read this chapter and discuss how you can all work together to keep the cash wrap looking fabulous.

STEP SEVEN: CHANGE IT

Your frequent shoppers visit the cash wrap often. Keep it interesting and ever changing, with new merchandise for last minute purchases and displays that reflect the season.

Don't let your cash counter look like the kitchen counter. Think of it as a perfectly set table, waiting to delight your guests.

9
Walk This Way

I love to look at stores and showrooms to discover ideas for displays, trends, and what's happening out in the world of retail. Of course, sometimes I am also buying shoes, but basically shopping is research for me. This has been a busy summer, and I have seen some terrific things; but I have also observed lots of fittings and fixtures in need of repair that shopkeepers don't seem to notice, even in stores that otherwise appear very well run. It is usually simple stuff—an occasional empty card rack, a desultory dust kitten, burned out bulbs, and my personal favorite, dead flies in the window.

You don't usually see all these things in one store (at least not where I like to shop), because most merchants pay attention to the details, but often elements slip through the cracks because we are all very busy and just don't see everything.

The trick is to *look* at your store. Do a walk-through of your store and really analyze it. This is not a new idea. It's not something I invented late one night to change the way we run our businesses and help us make zillions of dollars. It's an old idea, a technique that is essential to a well-run store. I think everybody knows about it, but WE FORGET TO DO IT!

MONTHLY

Set time aside to look at the store and make a list of what needs to be done. If you remember the last time you did this in your store, congratulate yourself and keep reading, just in case you missed something. If you don't remember your last walk-through, join the rest of us. It is understandable. Independent retailers have long to-do lists and a variety of disparate duties, from handling freight to doing displays. It is hard to stay on top of it all and so easy to become overwhelmed. No wonder we end up with dusty shelves or dirty windows.

A walk-through makes you focus on finding the things that need to be fixed or improved, displays that should be revamped, and product that could be moved. Every store has a thousand little chores waiting, from merchandise that is not on the floor and needs to be displayed to dirt that *is* on the floor and needs to leave. The problem is that once you start doing all these things, you become immersed and it is hard to prioritize.

You've probably seen a cluster of suited people, clipboards in hand, walking through a chain store someplace, all looking very serious, speaking in hushed tones and taking notes. That was probably a management group doing a walk-

Teach the staff

Take your staff for a tour of the store and show them how the shop should look. Teach them how to arrange merchandise on the shelves and racks, where the dust collects and how the displays are supposed to look. Sometimes an overview will help them pay more attention to the details.

through. While the chain stores may have the store manager, the display person, a few department heads, and a district manager or two doing a walk-through, you can do it by yourself or enlist a little aid.

Though you can go it alone, you will do a more thorough job if you have another person with you. A key staff member is great, but you could also ask another store owner or a rep whose judgment you trust to step in occasionally. Schedule your walk-through when you can concentrate, either before the store opens or when other staff members can take care of the customers. Start outside the front door and look at the windows, then come inside and really *stare* at your store. Think about what you see. Is the glass clean? Anything bad in the corners of the windows? Is your door clean? Are there too many posters lingering there? Are any of the flyers for events that are over? Which displays are looking shoddy? What dirt lurks on the floor? Don't fix it—list it. You'll take care of the problems later—this exercise is just to find them. Look at your displays extra carefully. Which have been in place for too long? What inventory is not selling and should be re-merchandised? Don't forget the stockroom. Is it well organized? Efficient? Clean? How about the bathroom?

Analyze your signage. Is it consistent and easy to read? Is there a sign in every place that customers may need an explanation? Are any of them faded, out of date, or tattered?

Is the carpet showing wear? Are there walls crying for new paint?

You want to analyze your store from front to back, top to bottom, inside and out, then plan the changes that need to be made and the chores that must be done. Also look at the parking lot and the sidewalk or mall in front of your store, since the entrance and what leads to it are parts of the first impression you give your customers.

After the walk-through, make a list of what needs to be done and when it should be accomplished. Some things will be critical (think "remove gum from sidewalk") while others may be more long-term goals (for instance, "replace gum display with new product line").

Especially after your first walk-through, you'll end up with a long list of things to address. Some you can take care of at once, others will take more planning. Big things, like new fixtures or lighting, may take months.

NOTICE THE GOOD THINGS

Don't forget to note the good things! Take digital pictures of good displays so you can re-work them for another season or use them again another year.

Very important: look at areas that your staff have kept clean, re-merchandised, or restocked, and tell them that you noticed and appreciate their efforts. Be lavish with your praise, as recognition and appreciation are key motivators for your employees—actually more important than their pay rate.

WEEKLY

Once a week, maybe Monday or Tuesday morning, take a quick tour of the shop and see what needs to be done that week. Check for empty shelves, displays that look tired, merchandise that needs to be counted for reorders, and dirt in all its many forms.

You don't have to do it yourself every week. If you make a form or checklist, one of your employees can look at the store and do the assessment. I think it is good to have different people perform this chore, since everybody notices different things.

Check the back room!

Always, always replace what you sell from the floor. Amazingly, the inventory in the warehouse does not turn as quickly as the merchandise on the floor. While we all have the best intentions about re-stocking, almost every store has a few things that are not out.

DAILY

I even have a quick daily walk-through list for the employee who opens the store. It is extremely simple, but truly helps to keep the store looking good—and to keep the staff *looking* at the store. It's simple: 1. areas to clean, 2. merchandise to restock, 3. displays to straighten, 3. back stock to tidy, 4. merchandise to count for reorder.

This list lives on a clipboard at the wrap desk, so any staff member can find a little project at any time. The clipboard is also where the staff puts notes or thoughts for my husband or me about displays that don't look good or repairs that need to be done.

TWICE A YEAR

These are the basic, everyday versions of a walk-through. Now let's go for the big guns. Once or twice (or four times) a year, get dressed up a little, go out to lunch someplace nice with another shopkeeper or someone who understands retail, and then go shopping.

Shop in other stores of various types and then *shop your own store*, looking around totally from a *customer's* viewpoint. Compare your impressions and observations. Is the staff friendly and attentive? Is the store appealing? Well-stocked?

Make notes about all the stores you visit, and see how you can improve your own shop. Spend time thinking about what you do well, also, so you continue to improve.

The time you spend shopping together should be fun, and you'll come home with a bag full of ideas for your own business. Maybe a new outfit, too.

Here's an easy way to help you keep your store in tip-top condition: make your walk-through a habit. Analyzing your store weekly or monthly will pay off in a better looking store and an improved bottom line.

Sometimes you have to step back to take a closer look …

10
Questions from the Audience

I have given presentations on a variety of topics ranging from how to write business plans to selling on eBay, and from how to move slow-selling merchandise to building your store's presence on the web. I have talked about display and trends, tweens and toddlers. The best part of the seminar circuit is meeting and talking with the retailers and learning more about what is happening in the real world of retail.

After almost every seminar, there are questions from the audience, some of which become the basis for columns or new seminars. Here are a few questions, with answers, from recent presentations.

WHERE DO YOU GET YOUR INSPIRATION?

This was asked after a seminar about display and merchandising, and it was my favorite question of the year because it really made me think. I love retail and find display unbelievably exciting. I am lucky enough to be able to spend lots of time looking for merchandising ideas and tracking trends, looking for ideas and trends that will help independent retailers. It is easy to find the ideas when you are looking for them, but they don't often pop right out at me while I am shopping for the kids or doing the laundry. Inspiration can be everywhere, but I think you have to be searching for it to recognize it

Make some time to look for ideas for your business. Start looking at presentation as well as product at the next trade show you attend. Do the same thing at the mall—go in early with the mall walkers and just look at the windows to see what props the professionals have used and how they are showing the goods. You can find display ideas in all types of stores, from produce stands to hardware stores, if you are in the right frame of mind to see it and figure out how to adapt what you see for use in your store.

I keep a notebook and a digital camera in my purse, so I can always record what I happen to find for later use.

I find inspiration at gift shows, showrooms and any place people shop, from flea markets to department stores. I look at the way merchandise is presented, how the store is laid out and the signage used. In one productive visit to a brand new grocery store I took notes about customer flow, methods of serving samples and the product descriptions on the prepared foods. The highlight of that trip was discovering that the blackboards in the produce department were magnet-friendly, a versatile and interesting surface for signage.

Thanks, Andrea

This column was edited by Andrea Grossman, a woman of letters as well as stickers. One of the many things I have learned from her is the importance of careful editing and proofreading on everything you do, from printed ads and your Web site to in-store signage. Have everything checked for grammar, spelling and content. Then check it again.

HOW OFTEN DO I NEED TO CHANGE MY DISPLAYS?

As often as you can! Redo something in your store every week, even if it is only a small section or one category. The window should change at least monthly. Naturally, any time you sell the focal point in a display, it has to be remerchandised. If you have a display that just didn't work or is getting no attention, change it immediately.

In the Mood for Inspiration

There are great ideas every place, all the time, but we are not always in the mood to see them. I find that while I occasionally stumble across something terrific, notice it an record the details, I am usually so busy thinking about whatever errands I am doing that I don't see things or get ideas every time I go shopping. However, when I really decide to look for inspiration and ideas, they are everyplace. This is a technique I honed at various home improvement and hardware stores while waiting endlessly for my husband to collect a basket full of practical but not very intriguing items.

WHAT ARE SOME REALLY CHEAP DISPLAY TRICKS?

My favorites:

Paint is the absolute cheapest way to transform anything in your store, from a fixture to a wall. Shop in the OOPS! paint section at your hardware store for an interesting color, put it on an area in the store, then build your entire presentation around it.

Vintage furniture from garage sales, flea markets, or the side of the road makes interesting display pieces and conversation starters. Keep your eye open for old tables, dressers, and chairs. It does not have to be great shape—a quick coat of paint will transform almost anything. Old bicycles are good, too.

Artificial flowers, fruits, and plants are very handy to have around to use in display. If you don't carry them, buy them on sale at the end of the season for next year. Be sure to keep them clean and throw them out when they are tired.

DO I REALLY NEED A WEBSITE? I DON'T PLAN TO SELL ANYTHING ON THE WEB.

YES!!! Every store needs a website, even it is just informational.

HOW MANY LINES DO I NEED TO CARRY?

There isn't a set number of lines—you need to have enough merchandise to sell in the store and to keep it looking good, whether it is from 20 manufacturers or 200.

WHAT IF I CAN'T MEET THE MINIMUM WITH A COMPANY?

Don't buy the line if you don't want enough of it to meet the minimum. Cherry pickers rarely prosper.

YOU SAID EVERYBODY WORKING IN THE STORE SHOULD WEAR APRONS OR SOME SORT OF UNIFORM. WHAT ABOUT MALE EMPLOYEES?

Men should wear aprons, too, preferably without ruffles.

CAN I SELL ANTIQUES OR VINTAGE ITEMS IN MY STORE ALONG WITH NEW PRODUCTS?

Absolutely! Antiques add lots of charm to a store—and at high margins. Be sure you clearly label antiques with their special information and mark reproductions so that your customers are not confused about what is old and what is new.

IS YOUR HUSBAND REALLY AS CHEAP AS YOU SAY HE IS?

Yes.

11
Idea Journaling

Merry Christmas! Happy Chanukah! Happy Kwanza! And a fabulous New Year to you! When the end of another year arrives, it's time for reflection and resolutions, and of course, a big sale. I'm sure you have the plans for your sale well under way, but what about your plans for next year? Take a little time to think about the past year and what you did right in the store. Take inventory of your successes! If you are still in business, with some money in the bank, after the last few years in retail, you have triumphed. Congratulate yourself!

Record your ideas

Always carry a digital camera and notebook with you in case you see something you can adapt for use in your store. I find ideas for the store, columns and seminars everywhere and try to keep notes so I will remember them later. I also clip ideas from lots of magazines. Unfortunately, instead of an organized journal or file, I dump them all in a big basket, which I do not recommend.

There's another reason to remember the things that worked well in your shop: you want to repeat that success. A terrific seasonal promotion will become an institution if you do it for a few years. In fact, it can be a tradition as early as the second year. A staff incentive that worked well bears duplication. Successful displays can be reworked for another use or different product.

We are often so busy thinking ahead and running behind that we have trouble coming up with the inspiration for the displays and promotions that are so important for our businesses. This brings us to my suggestion for your New Year's Resolution. It's easy, cheap, and simple: start (and then use) an Idea File and a Display Journal.

Most of us shop competing stores, read trade magazines, and talk to other merchants at trade shows. Then what happens? We get terrific ideas, tips, and inspirations which we are just positive we will remember and then forget at least half of them. Keep a notebook or recorder in your pocket, and write the ideas down.

In a pinch, call your home number from your cell phone and leave a message for yourself with the tip.

Clip articles from the trade magazines you read. I also save interesting information from consumer magazines and newspapers as well as my notes from seminars. If you are well organized, set up files by subject. If you are like me, dump them all in one file and go through them occasionally for ideas. Pictures are even more powerful. I have a digital camera that I carry in my purse so that I am always ready to take a shot for later use in a seminar. The great thing about digital photography is that you can take pictures of everything that interests you and then choose what you want to keep later. The point of this is to get inspired, so don't limit yourself to stores that are similar to yours. If you like a display, take the picture and then think about how to use it later. Often, it can be modified or adapted to work for the products you sell.

Inspiration begins at home. Take pictures of the windows and displays in your own store! You can repeat the good ones with new merchandise, different colors, or simply reproduce them a year or two later. Keep notes about the events you hold and the promotions you run. Some can be held annually, making them traditions, and some can be re-worked for another use. Repeating events are easy for customers to understand, too, since you have already trained them. The bonus is that each year your promotion will get better, since you've had practice; and it will be easier, since you've done it before.

Consider keeping a seasonal journal. Record ideas for windows, promotions, displays, and in-store events in chronological order so that you can look in your book or file for inspiration as each season approaches. Include everything that catches your eye—you can always weed it out later. One Halloween I went idea shopping and made notes about the products I saw, the colors (well, that wasn't tricky), the motifs and thought about who the target customer is. My conclusion? Pretty soon we won't think about kids at Halloween at all. The adults are having a great time dressing up.

I've taken pictures of the best windows at the mall, two or three great displays, terrific pumpkins, and some creative costumes that I saw at a downtown trick-or-treating event. I also made a few notes about popular costume themes ... did you notice an incredible number of infant Elvises in your area? Did the kids request those costumes or are their twenty- and thirty-something parents obsessed with The King?? Is there window potential here? Perhaps my town is just a faintly terrifying aberration. I'll put these notes and some articles from shelter magazines either in a file or in the box with my store's Halloween decorations so I can find them easily when it is time to dress and decorate next year.

Trade shows are full of fodder for your idea journal. Take a few hours to walk the show looking for display ideas rather than merchandise. Look everywhere, not just in the booths or showrooms where you usually shop. Take your notebook: not everyone allows photographs. Attend seminars. Scour the magazine bins and read periodicals from other industries—there are often excellent management or trend articles in them. Talk to the people you meet at the shows! Your fellow merchants have the best ideas and solutions you will find anywhere.

There are two points to the notebooks and files. The obvious one is that if you write an idea down, your chances of remembering it increase (or you can read it again).

Creative stimulation is the main reason for the display journal. You may flip through the photos and do a window that is very similar to one in the journal. The chances are even better that you'll look at the pictures, begin to get excited, and think of fabulous new ways to present product and merchandise your store.

Then you'll see people with cameras outside your windows. I might be one of them.

Time Your buying

Is your buying cycle correct? Are you ordering too much at a time and carrying too much inventory? With key vendors, you may find that ordering more frequently helps keep your inventory levels more manageable. While you do not want to carry too much product, always have enough so that you do not run out of essential items. Also, consider whether your order will qualify for discounts, dating or free freight. Sometimes it is worth ordering more for the increased margin.

II

Marketing and Promotion

12
Who Sets the Trends?

The gift industry is trend-driven, without a doubt. We are always searching for the Next Big Thing, worried that we are holding onto the Current Big Thing a little too long, terrified that we won't be able to sell the last three pieces of the Last Big Thing. And we've completely forgotten the Big Thing Before That, except for Beanie Babies, which makes us all heave a big sad sigh, either because we aren't selling them any more or because we missed the boat and didn't sell them at all.

Here's the deal. The Next Big Thing is usually not a trend. It is an item. A trend is a general direction, a movement of a large number of people. It is a trend to use brown in place of black this year. Pet Rocks and Big Mouth Billy Bass were not trends, they were items that had their moments in the sun and have now passed on to retail heaven. In short, Beanie Babies were an item. Collecting them was a trend.

Finding the Next Big Thing is important and certainly helps your bottom line, but recognizing trends and using them to influence your buying means more than item-hunting. You need to look at your customers and see what they are doing, wearing, and putting in their homes. Have you thought about the people shopping in your store? Try making a list of the ages and types or customers you have. Describe your top five archetype shoppers, their interests and lifestyles. The trends that should matter to you are those in your community.

If your core customers drive millions of miles per week in their mini vans and attend lots of soccer games, look for soccer mom stuff. Is there a large number of one ethnic group in the area? Look for product aimed at that demographic. Are your customers pregnant? Old? Married? Happily single? Are there lots of weddings in your community? Look around!

Fashion is a great place to look for trends. The colors, patterns, and looks on the runways this season will be seen on items in the gift shows soon. If all the teenagers are wearing monogrammed shirts and carrying purses with their initials on them, look for items with letters for their rooms. Look at the displays in the department stores and ready-to-wear shops.

Gift shows are another place to spot the trends. See what merchandise and colors are being featured by the reps and manufacturers for clues to the hottest developments in the business. Try to schedule a little time each market just to hunt for trend and display ideas.

Once you have found a few trends worth pursuing, buy enough merchandise to tell the whole story. Do a display with signage that tells your customers exactly what you are selling.

Two Little Words

Many of us ask the same thing in every booth at a show: "What's New?" we say brightly, expecting, but rarely getting, some fabulous new item to carry us through another season. For a better bottom line, start asking "What Sells?" or "What reorders?". Proven good sellers are a better bet than lots of new items without track records.

RECENT TRENDS

PET GIFTS

Dogs are loyal, devoted, true, and their owners (and their owners' friends) are buying more and more goodies for man's best friends. At the same time, cat owners are always trying to please their animals, so feline gifts are flying. Pet sales are multiplying like rabbits …

Trend tracking

I have spent hundreds of hours chasing trends, looking for great display and crawling malls for ideas for seminars and columns. Here are some of the places to look for trends:

Shelter magazines

Trade magazines

Popular magazines like People, Seventeen, and Vogue

Trade shows

Web newsletters

Stores of all types

E-mail newsletters

Seminars

LOVE IS IN THE AIR

Weddings, commitment ceremonies, and vow renewals are on the rise. Build (and promote!) a good gift registry and use it for all occasions.

HOME DÉCOR

People are still nesting and decorating their homes. Look for continued growth in this area, ranging from furniture to home accessories, pictures frames, and throw pillows.

HOME ENTERTAINING

Remember the "Cocooning" trend? Well, now the trend is "Hiving." That means bringing your friends into the home you so carefully decorated while you were cocooning. This trend is helping to increase sales of hostess gifts, gourmet foods, and invitations.

TWEEN SHOPPERS

Tweens, girls age 9–12, are shopping like crazy, and they are fun customers. They are looking for grown-up merchandise that still has a little girl quality to it. They love bright colors, lip gloss, and accessories for their rooms. These are the shoppers of tomorrow, so it is an important group.

CRAFTING

Thanks to Martha, we still want to be able to do it all. Sales continue to be strong in lots of segments of this market, including sewing, decorative painting, and quilting. The fastest rising trend in this area is knitting.

SCRAPBOOKING

This section of the market continues to show double digit increases. If you have a gift shop, tap into it with albums, frames, and scrapbooking kits. By the way, scrapbooking has created an interest in card making, which allows scrapbookers to use their tools, techniques, and even their left-over supplies in a new way.

Sports

Adults as well as children are playing more sports, especially soccer, tennis, and golf. In addition, there is a great market in people who are watching games at home (or in the stadiums). Look for licensed merchandise for these customers.

Book clubs

Books clubs are on the rise everywhere. Some stores have started their own book clubs with meetings in the store! This also works with home entertaining, since most book club meetings involve refreshments.

Value oriented buying

Consumers are willing to pay for quality, but they must understand the difference in products. Consider a Good Better Best promotion to demonstrate the quality differences in similar product. This is excellent for candles, pillows, and towels. Help customers make educated choices as they shop in your store!

Define your core products

What pays your rent? Which products bring your customers back again and again? Define what your customers depend on your store to carry and always be in stock. *Look for consumable items, like candles, personal care and food.*

Holidays

People are celebrating lots of holidays. Halloween is now a major season and Valentine's Day now extends past romance to friends and family. Make a big deal out of every holiday in your store.

In addition to thinking about what your customers are buying, think about how they are buying and where else they are shopping.

Check out the big guys! All the big box stores have chipped away at our market. Visit these stores and see what they are selling that is comparable to the merchandise in your store. If you carry similar product, be sure that your prices are competitive or that the difference is clearly evident. Good signage is an excellent way to state the benefits of your products clearly.

The biggest mistake you can make when following trends is to try to capitalize on too many at once. Little bits of lots of stories are not a good idea—your store will become confusing and disjointed.

Once you have defined a trend that you think will work in your store, buy enough of it to make a statement. Tell the whole story! Buy some bigger pieces to anchor the display and draw attention to the smaller items.

DON'T FORGET THE ROOSTERS!

Whatever you buy and however you display it, trends are only part of the story. You cannot stock a store on trend merchandise alone. You need core inventory, products your customers can depend on you to carry. Your store can be absolutely on-trend, but that doesn't necessarily mean you have what your customers want. While a shopper may come into the store because of your fabulous orange window and be delighted with your tribute to sixties modernism, if her kitchen is decorated with roosters, that is what she really wants to buy.

Defining, and refining, the inventory that you carry every day is the most important part of successful buying. Your store needs sufficient inventory on the merchandise that brings your customers back again and again. Fundamental categories like cards, candles, gourmet food, and personal care are fabulous because they engender a need in the customer; and consumable items will have to be replaced!

The basics are what keep you in business year after year, so be sure that you have the products your customers need and want. Jazz up your assortment with some new looks, add lots of current colors for pizzazz, but don't lose sight of the lines and merchandise your customers really want. You need the money.

13
Holiday Happenings:
Successful Ways to Stimulate Sales

November and December are busy and exciting times in almost every household. Starting in mid-October all the way to the end of the year, there are lots of occasions to enjoy and celebrate, from tailgate parties and Halloween to Chanukah, Christmas, and New Year's.

Your store's promotion calendar should be as full as Scarlett O'Hara's dance card to maximize your fourth quarter profits. The entire season should be all about excitement. Start planning promotions now that will make your store a destination. Naturally, your store will be full of great product and beautifully merchandised. Now you need to generate lots of excitement without breaking the bank. Begin planning your promotions early!

I once wanted to become an atheist, but I gave up —they have no holidays.

—Henny Youngman

HOLIDAY OPEN HOUSE

This is a classic fourth quarter promotion, and it is classic because it works. Invite your customers to a special event in mid-November, before the big rounds of parties begin, to get them excited about the holidays and ready to buy.

CHRISTMAS IS A TIME FOR GIVING

Acting as a drop-off point for your local food bank, Toys for Tots, or the Salvation Army will give new customers a reason to visit your store and give your regular customers another reason to drop in. Tell the story in your store window with an appropriate display, and be sure to send a press release to all local media.

TASTE OF THE HOLIDAYS

Do you sell food? Serve it! People often buy what they try, as anybody who has returned from Costco with a trunk full of unusual foods can attest. Even if you are not in the gourmet business, consider selling hot spiced cider mix. It smells great, makes a nice treat for the customers, and sells like crazy. Check out Christmas Wassail from Brownlow (www.brownlowgift.com).

GIFT WRAP GALA

If space permits, teach your customers how to wrap gifts and tie bows. Make it an evening event, serve snacks, and invite representatives from the gift wrap companies you carry to show their expertise. If it is a hands-on class, charge a class fee and give them lots of product to work with. Ask your vendors for help planning the class. It can also be a dandy charity event with a percentage of the proceeds going to a local cause.

LET IT SNOW … FLOW PACK

What do you do with all the excess packing materials from the merchandise you receive? Give them away, I say. Your customer will be thrilled with a garbage bag full of flow pack, tied with a ribbon. You won't have to pay to throw it away, and it is an easy way to recycle. Do the same with bubble wrap—roll or fold it and tie it with jute, string, or ribbon. Add a tag that tells why you are giving this away, put your logo on it, and it is a great gift for your shopper that costs you almost nothing. The downside is that this may become difficult to store, but once your customers get wind of it, it won't last long.

Every Day's a Holiday

We always think of December as the only time for holidays. Well, it's not. Celebrate every holiday in your store … and make up a few when you run out of the standards. Your customers come to you for entertainment and interest and a celebration of any kind, however silly, is always fun.

HOLIDAY CHECK LISTS

Help your customers shop by telling them what to buy for specific types of people. Post framed lists in the store with titles like "What Men Really Want," "Make a Tween Happy this Holiday," "Thoughtful Hostess Gifts" (and so forth), and then list the items you recommend for them. Have your staff help you make the lists so they are as comprehensive as possible.

MUSICAL MERRY CHRISTMAS

Music is an important mood-setter in the store. In addition to the recorded music (which you should sell, by the way), think about having carolers or a children's choir perform during your holiday events. Live entertainers add a lot to a party and can often be found at a reasonable price.

WHAT ABOUT THE CHILDREN?

Kids love to be treated like adults and a holiday open house just for them is a great way to build business with your future consumers. Hold the open house on a Saturday morning, offer cookies and punch, and free gift wrapping. This will require a collection of lower priced items that they can afford. Another option is to have events where the kids make gifts for their parents. This pays off well—while the kids are doing the craft, the mothers are shopping.

DON'T FORGET THE PETS!

Santa loves dogs and cats almost as much as he loves good children, even dogs who eat his cookies and cats who drink his milk. See if you can schedule Santa for a Saturday morning to have his picture taken with the good animals in the neighborhood.

GIFT CERTIFICATES FOR YOUR TOP CUSTOMERS

Here's a new twist on a loyalty program: send your 100 top customers a thank you note and a gift certificate for $20.00 to be spent before the end of the year. You will absolutely delight your very best customers by sending them gifts, with no strings attached, that they can spend in the store. While it may seem expensive, it is actually not a bad deal at all. Your cost of goods for a $20 gift is about $11.00 (based on a keystone markup and adding 10% freight), which is not much to thrill a good customer. You've chosen your top shoppers, so you know that when she comes in she'll spend far more than face value of the coupon.

☙

Here's the most important bit of advice in this chapter. Whatever you do, promote the heck out of every single event. Send press releases to all media in your area. Let the TV station know that Santa is entertaining animals at the store. Make sure the radio stations know that Toys for Tots can be dropped off at your store. !

Mail (or email) your customers a holiday newsletter that tells them about the fun they can have at your store. Mention every service you perform: gift wrapping, coat checking, and gift registry, for instance.

The holidays are a great time to build your mailing list. Provide a guest book to sign or cards to fill out, so customers can provide their addresses and emails in order to be informed about new merchandise and invited to special events and private sales. Perhaps hold a prize drawing with the cards.

One little note: margin is king all year long, including Christmas, so remember that markdowns are not promotion! Marketing techniques to watch carefully are frequent-shopper discounts, punch cards, and similar programs. If you are not careful, you end up taking 10–20% off the top of your very best sales. An independent retailer cannot compete with the big guys on price, so you must rely on your creativity and the uniqueness of your store.

Give yourself a break

I was behind deadline, with lots of writing ahead of me when I received a call from a neighbor. He had two tickets to the Radio City Rockettes for a show that was starting in ninety minutes and wondered if my husband I and would like to see it. Naturally, I said I had to work on my book, my husband was working at the store and we could not possibly take the time off for something as frivolous as a show.

Then I saw my daughter's face and realized I had made a big mistake. I called him back, Keara and I got dressed up, went out, had a great time and then I stayed up really late writing. Having a special evening with my twelve year old was much more important than the sleep I missed.

Retailers work hard. Give yourself time for a little fun.

14
Wrap This!!

Gift wrapping is highly targeted direct marketing. Every beautifully wrapped present that bears your store's logo is an advertisement for your shop. While it is seen only by the giver, the recipient, and perhaps a few party guests (well, maybe a few hundred if you're really lucky and the present goes to a big wedding), people remember the gifts they give and receive and how they were presented. A fabulous wrap job makes the present look important and special. I have a friend who has had a gift in her living room for about five years that she won't open because it is so gorgeous (I hope it's not perishable).

Gift wrapping is a marketing expense, not a store supply expense. It is not required. It is a bonus for your customers, a reward for shopping in your store. It is another way to bring your customers to the store and keep them coming back. Planned correctly, free gift wrapping is a terrific benefit for you and your customers.

Before you start looking at pretty ribbons, analyze your business. Will your margins support the additional costs? Is your average sale high enough? If your store operates on short markups or your average sale is low, you can't afford this luxury. My husband, in business for 28 years, never offered gift wrapping. He told the few customers who complained that he would help them wrap their gifts: then he sold them tote bags, tissue, and ribbon and wrapped the gift for them. Another important issue is time—do you have the staff to handle the wrapping? Can you be sure they are trained to wrap nicely and efficiently? Wasted wrapping materials are extremely expensive.

Here's an example of the wrong way to do it: I had a gift wrapped in a major chain bookstore. The saleslady used half again too much paper, about five times too much tape and took a long time. There was no ribbon or decoration of any kind, but most important, there was no sticker. She forgot to include their custom bookmark with the book, so there was no store identification anywhere. I appreciated the effort, but the job was sloppy and incomplete; and I actually rewrapped the book. What did that store gain? Nothing. I was irritated because she was incompetent and slow, the package looked terrible, and there was no brand identification. Great gift wrapping is an added value, but a shoddy job adds no value and does not enhance your store's image—it's even bad advertising!

Gift wrapping is part of creating your store brand. *Every single package you wrap must have your store name on it!* This is non-negotiable. You provided the gift wrap; you deserve the credit on the box. Whether you use imprinted boxes (foil stamping can cost as little as ½ cent per box) or custom stickers, this is an absolute necessity. (Scrapbookers sometimes incorporate such store stickers

Basic Skills

Your staff may not know how to wrap gifts ... or they may use so much paper, tape, ribbon and time that it costs you a fortune. Teach them exactly what you want them to do and how to do it. If you use paper to over-wrap, show your wrappers how to use the paper most efficiently, so there is as little waste as possible. Ribbon tying is not hard, but it is a skill that requires practice.

If you do not know how to do wrap quickly, efficiently, and frugally, hire a professional wrapper to come in give your staff a class.

into layouts that celebrate the event and the gift received. So your little sticker may go on marketing for years!)

Gift wrapping, like any form of advertising, builds future business. While you may not see the immediate effect on your bottom line, this service is another way to make your store special and set yourself apart from the big stores.

Some stores offer a variety of wraps or change their looks frequently. This is a logical approach since it gives you the opportunity to buy closeouts, overstocks, and special purchases, and there is a lot of very well-priced gift wrapping material available. It is also fun for your staff to have new papers and supplies. If you do vary your store wrap, your label becomes extremely important. It should be well designed (your store logo is a good idea) and positioned carefully on the package. No crooked labels, please!

While switching wrap styles may be more cost efficient, my feeling is that you should have a signature wrap that evokes the ambiance of your store. You will effectively brand your store with a gift wrap that is consistent (so your customers learn to recognize it) and clearly shows your store name. Within a basic design scheme, you can change colors or add decorations as needed, but always keep the same feeling. You'll know you've done it right when customers say, "She'll be so excited as soon as she sees your box!" I firmly believe that anyone should be able to identify your store's gifts at 50 paces. Changing your gift wrap style is almost as important as changing your logo and should not be done casually. Think of Nordstrom or Crate and Barrel. Gifts from these stores are immediately identifiable. Customers even develop sentimental attachment to a store's gift wrap. Think of the visceral reaction a Tiffany's box can evoke. Bonwit Teller's is gone, but their delicate violets live on in the memories of many. Tap into that emotional appeal with your own gift wrap identity!

Whether you create a consistent style or have an array of gift wrapping choices for your customers, you'll also need to plan the place in your store for wrapping and make the project as well regimented and organized as you can. Dedicate a wrap center and have all the supplies at hand. Have training sessions with your staff. If your gift wrap is really fabulous, show samples in your displays to encourage your customers to buy a gift.

A gift isn't really a gift until it is wrapped. Offering this service is a great help to your customers and excellent advertising for you. Think of those wrapped packages as little ambassadors of good will from your store.

Do you want that scent?

When wrapping something soft, suggest that the customer add a bar of scented soap to the package—it will give the gift a nice aroma when the lucky recipient opens it. You can also add a very tiny amount of potpourri for the same effect.

15
The Nitty Gritty of Wrap

When you design and shop for your store wrap, arm yourself with the right information. You need to know:

> your average sale so you can budget for the expense
>
> the approximate sizes and shapes of items you will wrap most often so you can choose the appropriate boxes or bags. (Too big an assortment of supplies can easily become confusing and messy.)
>
> the occasions you need to consider. The three most common themes needed for gift wrap are everyday, wedding, and holiday, but your store may have special needs. (If possible, try to change just the ribbon, tissue or the tie-on to customize the packages for different events.)

With this basic information, you will be able to buy more effectively. Clyde Brownstone, president of Gift Box Corporation of America says "Be prepared! It is helpful to know what color theme you have in mind before you start to shop. Bring color swatches of your walls, carpets, and signs so you can match them to your packaging. Have your logo with you so you can visualize your name on the boxes and bags. Don't make this the last stop at the mart. Ordering custom imprinted boxes and bags takes a little more time than buying product."

BOXES

High quality gift boxes imprinted with your store name is the place to start. A box in the right color (or laminated with wrap) needs no overwrapping, just ribbon and gift tag. Hot stamping from Gift Box starts at only 1.5 cents per box, which is less than most labels. Their starter set comes in the seven most popular sizes.

Hupaco offers gift-ready boxes with folding bottoms and rigid lids, giving the appearance of set-up boxes at less than half the cost. Even less expensive are their telescoping "wrapped and ready" gift boxes, with folding tops and bottoms.

Laminated set-up boxes are another option. "These boxes have an archival quality—they are not throw-aways. The stores find there is tremendous residual advertising when they print their name inside the lid," says Richard Wilk, C.E.O. of Hupaco.

BAGS

Tote bags or colored lunch bags are an easy and quick method of wrapping soft

Branding

Your store wrap is part of the brand you are building. Make it distinctive, pretty and clearly labeled. Don't change patterns or colors often—your customer will learn to recognize you store's signature wrap. Make a statement and stick with it.

After all, Tiffany isn't looked for a new hue of blue for their boxes.

goods or smaller items. Clear or frosted poly bags are well priced, water-resistant, strong, and combine beautifully with colored or patterned tissues. Hupaco has some great patterns as well as a collection with macramé style handles.

COUNTER WRAP

You need good design, quality paper, and a competitive price. Cheap wrapping paper is a false economy. It tears easily, you can see through it, and it is hard for a novice to use. Paper is available in a variety of widths, with 24" generally the most convenient. "Buy a 30-inch cutter," suggests Richard Wilk. "You can use it for 24, 26, or 30 inch paper as you buy different rolls." He also recommends cutter boxes and half-ream rolls for seasonal or special occasion wrap. Another option if you wrap many boxes of the same size is Hupaco's sheeted paper, packed in cassettes.

TISSUE

Tissue has become an important and fun part of the wrapping process. There are now over 50 colors of solids as well as thousands of prints available. Use tissue to customize packages for the holidays. "It is an easy and inexpensive way to change your look without spending a lot of money," comments Pete Shore, director of marketing of the Gift Box Corporation.

"Custom printed logo tissue is available in quantities as low as ten reams. Plate costs have come down with the new technologies to make it available to smaller shops," adds Richard Wilk. "Another way to save money is to interleave it with white tissue."

RIBBON

There are so many ways to decorate a package! Sheer and wired ribbons are very, very popular, tulle is hot, raffia has been a staple for many years ... the choices seem endless. You can use a little as an accent on a small gift or really go all out for a special gift. Tie-ons can make a package almost magical, and there is no limit to what you can use, from sticks and feathers to small Christmas ornaments. A treat on the top of the gift is a great add-on sale, by the way.

Hupaco's cream city ribbon is a bonded cotton ribbon that is available in small quantities printed or hot stamped with your store name. It can be crimped into a grosgrain pattern, it is the best curling ribbon on the market, and it is all natural. There are 26 colors of threads on the palette that can be combined any way you wish.

Too Busy?

If the shop is busy and your customers have to wait for a long time for their packages to be wrapped, give them the option of returning later or even the next day to pick up the gifts. This is a time saver for them, frees you to help other customers and gives the lady a reason to come back to the store for a return visit.

LABELS

This is a key element! Use your store labels inside the box on the tissue as well as on the outside of every package. The ideal is to have a custom sticker made in the shape of your logo, but even if you settle for the simple gold variety, use them liberally. A quick hint: an oval or round sticker is easier to position than an oblong or square.

THE GIFT WRAP CENTER

Dedicate an area in the store for your wrap center. Organized supplies and tools make the job simpler and more efficient and help you stay abreast of what must be ordered. Have a sturdy tape dispenser, good scissors, and a clear working area.

Teach your employees how to wrap, and give the precise parameters for each type of gift. This is not an area for self-expression: your store image is serious business and must be consistent. Have "gift wrap school" for your staff and teach them how to tie bows and exactly what to use to wrap a gift neatly and without waste. Impress on them how important it is that the gifts you wrap look professional. Ugly presents are bad for business.

Don't set a minimum purchase for free gift wrapping. If you gift wrap, do it all and the average will work out. Recently I purchased six small bottles of olive oil at the Carmel Bay Company, in Carmel, California. Although they were only $5.50 each, the clerk offered to wrap them individually, which thrilled me beyond measure. The simple and inexpensive wrap job (tissue and raffia) was great looking and made a customer (me) and her five friends very happy and anxious to return.

The salespeople who sell packaging are usually very well versed in their products. Use their expertise! They'll have very helpful suggestions and ideas as you plan your presentation.

Fabulous gift wrapping is a gift that keeps on giving. Giving right back to you, the retailer.

See sources for gift wrap manufacturers.

16
Please Mr. Postman!

Here it is … the quiet time. The sleepy, post-holiday, pre-spring, dreary, gray time in retail. Now is when your customers need a little boost, a special event or a sale or a big announcement. What is the best way to get the word out to the people who really want to shop in your store? You contact them using the names on your mailing list.

Absolutely the most effective (and least expensive) promotion for independent retailers is direct mail. The list you build from the customers who shop in your store is a dedicated cadre of consumers who have already shown interest in your products. These people care enough to fill out the cards to add their names to the list. They know your store and like what you sell. They want to hear from you!

Planning an effective program of mailing and emails is the best use of your marketing dollars. The first step is accumulating names. Take advantage of the calm this spring to begin planning and organizing your mailing list.

DEVELOPING YOUR MAILING LIST

The first step is planning your list. While you can use a guest book, many customers don't want their names seen by others and will not sign. It is worth the investment to print attractive cards asking for all the information you will need to serve your customers better. Reflect your logo or gift wrap motif in the design of the card.

The basics (pretty obvious, I know) are name, address, phone, and email.

Follow this with: birthday, anniversary, spouse's name and birthday, children's names and years of birth. Now you have a profile of your customer's family and can tailor mailings with offerings appropriate to any member.

Now think about your store and the merchandise in your inventory. Think of the important merchandise classifications as well as the name brands you carry. Add a check-off list of important categories or lines so you can notify your customers when you get a big shipment, have a sale, or plan an in-store event. Your customers will appreciate the inside track on the information, and your sales will increase accordingly.

Table top stores should add a space for the customer to list her china, silver, and crystal patterns.

Any store carrying collectibles should list the brands they carry and allow their customers to check off the lines they collect (Dept. 56, Hummel, Precious Moments, etc.). These collectors are a prime group for dedicated mailings.

Handwriting counts

Nothing, absolutely nothing, beats a handwritten note. Encourage your staff (and yourself) to write thank you notes to your customers, send birthday cards or just drop a line about new products.

Ask yourself what is important to your customers and unique to your store as you develop the cards.

Email marketing

For more information about building an email marketing program and information about how to make it work, visit the friendly folks at OverCoffee Productions (overcoffee.com).

ORGANIZE YOUR LIST

Invest in contact management software like ACT or Access. These programs are amazingly easy to use and enable you to enter the information and sort by any of the criteria on your cards. It is fabulous! You will be able to send birthday cards at the right time, anniversary reminders, and notices that are directed specifically to the customers who will respond.

Learn to use the software as you plan the sign-up cards so you have the right information in the right places for ease of entry and use. Have the categories on the cards listed in the same order as the fields on the computer for ease of entry. If the computer program baffles you, take an adult education class or a course at the computer store near you. These programs are worth the time it takes to learn them and really quite easy to use once you get going. While the organization process is a hefty project, the time spent now will pay off as you use the list.

ADD A WISH LIST

If you keep the computer in the store and your employees have access to the database, keep a wish list for your customers so that anyone can choose a present that will be truly appreciated. You can add this to the cards your customers fill out or have a separate log. The Wish List works just like a wedding registry, but is not limited to brides. This is a terrific and much appreciated service to provide for the bewildered husbands or for the people who come in saying, "My friend has everything! What could she possibly want?"

MAINTAIN THE LIST

Always include dates when you add or update the entries on the list. It is also good to record responses to the mailings when you can (coupons redeemed, for instance) so you will know what got the customer's attention.

Don't waste your postage! Remove addresses from any returned items immediately and plan to purge your list every three years or so. I am still getting three to four mailings a year from a store in San Francisco (I live in Michigan now) which I haven't even visited since 1988.

E-MAILINGS

E-mailings are becoming more and more successful for independent retailers, especially used in conjunction with regular mailings. Get those addresses! Two quick notes; always include an option to be removed from the list and be sure your store is clearly identified when you send the e mails.

This is the beginning, a springtime start for a program that will blossom into sales later. Just like a garden, a great direct mail program requires planning, nurturing, and patience in addition to creativity and hard work. Happy Planting!

17
The Power of the Press Release

Hey Mary Liz,

The release came out and within hours we've gotten response from local papers and radio/TV stations! I've also been getting pitches from PR firms and interest from more stores around the country!

It's exciting and scary all at the same time. I think I know what you mean by media assault now. Wow, marketing is so important!

Sue Rostvold
Verysupercool
Austin, Texas 78704
www.verysupercool.com

Your local newspaper wants to hear from you, and it's not just the carrier looking for a tip. Your store is full of stories waiting to be told, announcements waiting to be made, and knowledge waiting for you to share. Reporters and columnists want to write about local news; their editors want to provide it to their readers. And you can help provide that information. Your store, regardless of size, annual sales, or advertising budget, is part of the community, and the events in your shop are newsworthy. Coverage in the local media is absolutely the best way to bring new and old customers into your store, and it is easy to get with a little practice and some effort.

Sending a press release is not the same as placing an ad. When you place an ad, you have total control of the content, and you pay for the placement. When you announce the events in your store, you are sharing *news* with people who want to know about it. The paper can use it exactly as you wrote it, re-write it, or completely ignore it, as they see fit. The advertising and editorial staffs of all media are separate and distinct—you cannot buy coverage. At any rate, you can't buy it from a reputable paper or magazine.

Your local papers are looking for information about products, promotions, and events offered by the local businesses. Sending a press release is helpful and kind and almost a public service. Ask any journalist you happen to see—we *love* press releases!

Debra Gold, president of Gold & Company, a leading strategic marketing and public relations firm in the gift and home industries, states: "Press releases are a simple, inexpensive, easy-to-use, professional tool that any retailer can use to stimulate sales, reach out to existing and new customers, "brand" your business as a great product resource in the community, and help make your store stand out from your competition. With a little practice, this one effective way to communicate your store's news and information could be magical for your profit potential!"

I am sure you have seen plenty of press for the big chain stores in your local papers. They get the coverage because they send the releases. It could, and should, be your store in those articles; and fortunately for us, most writers prefer to write about local businesses and independent merchants.

So how do you do it? As you set out to become the press relations specialist for your store, your twin goals are to build relationships with the press and share your knowledge and news with their readers and listeners.

BUILD YOUR LIST

As you read papers and magazines, start collecting the names of the reporters and make notes about what each of them covers. Include radio and TV reporters, too. Focus on local publications in particular. Get to know the writers! Meet them if you can, call them occasionally. Marketing to the media is as important as marketing to your top customers.

DEFINE YOUR TARGETS

As you think about promoting something, decide who is likely to write about it. Learn what each writer covers so you can target the right people with your information. Don't send a release about a fabulous new collection of pet merchandise to the garden editor. Ask yourself, "Is this news she can use?" before you send it, and your placement chances will increase.

DECIDE WHAT TO SAY

A press release is not an advertisement. You are telling a story, not selling a product. Always ask yourself what the *reader* cares about. The increased sales you will realize from the publicity you receive are a bonus, so think of the tale you are telling and the sales will follow. Read the articles and interviews with other store owners and business people and see what gets mentioned and why. One more thing: if you have nothing to say, do not send a press release. Flooding inboxes with pages and pages of nonsense is not the way to any writer's heart.

LEARN THE FORMAT

There is a basic format for press releases.

1. Your contact information goes at the top of the page. Include your name, business names, phone, and email address. This makes it easy for the writer to find you with his questions.
2. Put "For Immediate Release" below your contact info, so the writer knows that this is something to be used at once.
3. Skip three lines, then put the title in bold or larger type, centered on the page. Make that title snappy! This is where you catch the journalist's (and the reader's) attention.
4. Begin the first paragraph with the city and date.
5. Double space the copy (or 1.5 spaced). Make it fit on one page if humanly possible. This is roughly 400 words.
6. Who, What, When, Where, and Why are the questions to answer in the first paragraph. If you can answer the journalist's list of basic questions, you have covered it.

Be Bold, Brazen and Brave

Do you have an idea for a story for your local newspaper? A lead for a TV reporter? Go ahead! Propose it, send it in, give it a try. Reporters want to know what is happening around town, so tell them about upcoming events in your store, promotions you are about to run and new items that you are carrying. It is inexpensive and it really works. Keep writing. Not only will you get better with practice, but you'll build relationships with the members of the media. The worst that can happen is they ignore your release or proposal. Don't let that deter you: try again.

7. Add the details in the following paragraphs. If you have a quote from an expert or someone famous, like Debra Gold, add it as well. Remember that most editors will cut from the bottom of a release, so put the most important things at the top.
8. The final paragraph should contain the basic information about your store: a description or very short history, address, website, phone, and hours of operation. Save this paragraph—you can use it in every release.
9. Add contact information at the end. This is for the reader, not the writer, so it may not be the same person as the contact at the top of the page.
10. *Proofread* before sending. Also ask someone else to proofread before sending. Look for spelling and grammar mistakes, check clarity, and correct factual errors. Then proof it again. Trust me on this.

POLISH YOUR WRITING!

Write it, rewrite it, wait a day, and write it again. Good writing requires practice, and you want your copy to be excellent. I suggest you start with an outline of what you want to say and then add the details, stopping when you fill the page, or before.

WHAT TO TALK ABOUT

New product line or category introductions, milestones like grand openings, anniversaries, expansions or number of customers served, class schedules, trend information, and news (think scrapbooking, home entertaining, book clubs, or any kind of collecting). When publicizing charity events or promotions, tell the story about the charity and include details about where the money you raise will go.

CONTACT YOUR MANUFACTURERS

Ask your key vendors if they have press releases written for consumer publications. You can provide a press list to the company. They can send the information directly to the editors in your area, listing your store as the resource, or they may let you use their copy which you can submit yourself.

Once you get started writing your releases, make it a habit. They won't all get used, but when one hits, you will be thrilled and delighted at the increase in traffic … and sales.

III

❧

Meetings, Markets and Mingling

18

Talking in the Halls

Recently someone attending one of my seminars asked how I do research at markets. She was interested in finding trends and hot items. I told her that for many years I have found fabulous information at almost every show while I am waiting in line for the ladies room, at the hot dog stand, or on a shuttle bus. I certainly work the showrooms, read the trades, and collect the catalogs; but it is from the retailers in the stores and the reps on the street that I find lots of the most up-to-date and interesting information.

There is no greater knowledge base for store owners than other retailers. Whatever your question, any source you seek, any problem you need solved, there is another merchant who has the answer. Actually, there are several retailers with the answer. You just have to locate them.

So where do you find the people with the answers? At home, join a local merchant's association or service group. When you are at a trade show, talk to strangers. Come early and stay a little longer at seminars, and talk with the other attendees. Go to the parties and special events, and always sit with a stranger on the bus. Talk to reps and sales managers about more than the product they sell. Salespeople are talking to retailers all over their territories and have tons of knowledge.

Unusual shopping tip

Few people have done as many shows as New York rep Alan Spigelman. He maintains that one of the best ways to find out which are the hot items in a booth is to ask what has been taken. "They never take the slow sellers" he says, "In fact, I consider it an excellent sign when samples get stolen."

NATIONAL STATIONERY SHOW

The National Stationery Show is a goldmine for information. This show is a great source for new colors, motifs, and trends and is attended by retailers and reps from across the country. There are also many new companies debuting at this show, such as the very fashionable new line from Dallas called Three Designing Women. www.threedesigningwomen.com

While you are at the Stationery Show, don't miss the Gift for Life Gala. It is an unparalleled networking event and a great party. In addition, 100% of the money we raise goes to amFAR, supporting AIDS education and relief.

WALKING AND TALKING

I find more than information in the halls and on the busses. I find inspiration and excitement. After talking to other people in the industry, I get excited about my own business. Nobody really understands a retailer's life as well as another merchant. Spend a little more time with people who understand you.

Take your questions to market with you

When you make your list for a trade show, include questions you would like to ask another retailer. Whether you meet people at a seminar, in a networking event (have you joined It's Another?) or in the line for hot dogs, you may just find the person with the knowledge you seek. I have met many people and learned quite a lot waiting for the ladies room at Javits Center.

While I was in the halls in Columbus, I met Betty Plunkett, of Purchasing Power Plus, the nation's premier hospital gift shop buying group. She is starting a new buying group for independent retailers, which can be a terrific opportunity to increase your margins, with discounts, preferred terms, retail support, newsletters, website access, and more. Visit www.retailadvantagegroup.com and www.purchasingpowerplus.com for information about the rapidly-growing programs.

My 13-year-old son, Kegan Scannell, was with me at the spring market in Dallas. He helped at the seminars, worked the halls with me, and rode a mechanical bull at the Fort Worth Stockyards. After two days at the World Trade Center, I asked him if he enjoyed coming to work with his mother. Quite frankly, I was fishing for a compliment. His reply? "You don't actually work, Mom. All you do is walk around and talk to your friends all day."

Well, he's right. That is exactly what I do at market. If I were reporting to someone, I would say I had been researching or investigating. I might describe what I do as networking, if I didn't hate the term. But the truth is, I am talking to my friends. Some are friends I've known for many years and others are friends I am just about to meet.

19
Join Something (Out and About)

Do you belong to a club, society, association, or group that benefits your business? (Warehouse membership clubs don't count.) There is a trade organization for almost every sort of business and merchant's groups in nearly every locale. The members of these associations benefit from the educational, networking, and financial opportunities they provide.

TRADE ORGANIZATIONS

I have presented programs for a variety of trade organizations. Their conventions were organized by the professionals who run the group, with tremendous input and work from volunteer members. The result, in all cases, was a meeting filled with information, opportunity, and chances to meet others in the field. In each case the attendees found the expense of the trip well worth the money.

Most important, at every one of these were other members of the group. The programs they presented were worth the trip, having a chance to talk with leaders in the field is priceless.

CRAFT AND HOBBY ASSOCIATION (CHA)
www.hobby.org

The first was the Craft and Hobby Association (formerly known as the Hobby Industry Association). CHA's purpose is best summarized by its mission, "To stimulate the sales growth of the craft and hobby industry." Their annual show is the major international source for products in the craft and hobby industry. If you want scrapbooking supplies, craft tools of any kind, floral supplies, needlecrafts, framing materials, art materials ... CHA is the place to shop. But CHA is not just a show. It is a convention, with seminars, workshops, and classes that start early each day and last until well after midnight. Every buyer in the craft industry is there, from chains like Michaels to independent store owners—and they talk to each other.

The extensive educational program covers product use, business practices, and more. A week at this show is like a semester in Craft College—over 260 hours of instruction is common. In addition, CHA promotes tremendous national publicity for the craft industry.

GREETING CARD ASSOCIATION (GCA)

The Greeting Card Association is an organization representing greeting card and stationery publishers and allied members of the industry. Their mission

National Speakers Association

I am proud to be a member of the National Speaker's Association as well as the Michigan chapter of NSA and I attend every event I can. In addition to the skills I have honed and the tips I have picked up, the fact that I can spend time with other speakers, who know what the job is like and can talk and laugh about it is invaluable. Like retail, speaking can be a lonely business, even though you meet lots of lovely people.

Join a trade group or organization for the fellowship. You will be glad you did.

57

Host a Club

How about hosting a group in your store? If you have room for the Chamber of Commerce to meet or a book club to convene, invite them to the store. Many groups are looking for new and interesting venues for parties and meetings.

states: "The GCA celebrates, promotes, and protects the tradition and cultural values of exchanging greeting cards."

Like many wholesale trade organizations, the GCA provides trend information, promotes the category nationally, and is extremely active in Washington, lobbying on postal issues. These are the people who protected colored envelopes! This group also sponsors the LOUIE Awards, the greeting card industry's version of the Oscars. The GCA meeting is not a trade show, but an educational and networking opportunity for its members, large and small. About 100 people attended one recent GCA meeting, so it was an unbelievable opportunity for owners of small and emerging companies, like Meg McComb of Nutmeg Unlimited, to meet and talk with people from larger, established companies like John Beeder, Senior Vice President and General Manager Greeting Cards at Hallmark. Big and small, they had a chance to address common concerns and problems.

The GCA convention is not a cheap weekend by any means, but everyone I asked said it was worth every penny. As they say at the GCA, they've been "making every occasion special since 1941."

SOCIETY OF AMERICAN FLORISTS (SAF)

The Society of American Florists has absolutely the best smelling convention you'll ever attend. This group of about 500 meets for seminars and a floral competition featuring new varieties and to honor industry leaders. A beautiful, flower-filled weekend includes small and large companies gathering to exchange ideas, sources, and techniques. Plus, the centerpieces at the dance were beyond fabulous.

STATE RETAILER'S ASSOCIATION

Where do you get your credit card service? Workman's compensation insurance? Almost every state has a retailer's or merchant's organization with a vast array of benefits for members. Check out the organizations near you for these and other services.

LOCAL MERCHANT'S ASSOCIATION

Get to know your neighbors! Local merchant's groups plan promotional events like art fairs and sidewalk sales; they work with the city government on zoning and parking issues; and they work with each other to increase business. Additionally, when you make friends with the neighboring businesses, you have opportunities to cross-merchandise products and send each other business. Besides, it's nice to have someplace to go when you run out of tape or bags.

Gift Sales Managers Association
www.giftsalesmanagers.com

The Gift Sales Managers Association is a fairly new group, the only organization created by, and for, gift and home sales managers. I spoke at their conference and found a group that is dedicated to helping each other with specifics and enhancing the industry in general. Their mission is "to grow the industry by responding to the needs of our customers, rep groups, and industry peers through education and communication."

The GSMA is actively working to raise the level of professionalism in our business, improve communication and relationships with their sales representatives, and promote the well being of the independent retailer. In short, they're trying to make a difference in the gift industry. And they are succeeding.

Anyone in sales management in our industry will benefit from membership. Hurry! Membership is limited to 100 non-competing lines and is now about two-thirds full. If you are a sales rep or a retailer, visit the website to learn more about this worthwhile organization.

You don't have to join an organization to enjoy benefits from the work it does. Some groups have very strict admission policies, so you can't join them, but you should be aware of these organizations and what they do behind the scenes for your business. The Greeting Card Association has helped every store that sells greeting cards. The CHA has promoted tremendous public awareness of the craft industry, which has worked to the advantage of every store that sells craft kits of any kind.

When you do find a society that is focused on your business, join the club. Attend the meetings! Go to the seminars. Most important of all, talk to everyone at the gatherings. You'll make friends who understand the challenges in your industry and will share ideas and solutions to common problems.

Besides, they need you and your expertise, too.

Here are a few organizations to get you started:

American Booksellers Association
www.bookweb.org

Founded in 1900, the American Booksellers Association is a not-for-profit organization devoted to meeting the needs of its core members of independently owned bookstores with retail storefront locations through advocacy, education, research, and information dissemination. The ABA actively supports free speech, literacy, and programs that encourage reading.

American Specialty Toy Retailing Association (ASTRA)
www.astratoy.org

Provides an opportunity for specialty toy retailers, manufacturers, and sales representatives to come together to strengthen and expand the specialty toy market.

CALIFORNIA STATE FLORAL ASSOCIATION
www.calstatefloral.com

California organization representing the entire floral industry on a state level, supported by growers, wholesalers, retailers, and allied industries.

GIFT ASSOCIATION OF AMERICA
www.giftassoc.org

Founded in 1952, the Gift Association of America is the oldest and largest trade association comprised of retail stores and wholesalers in the gift industry. Established primarily to provide a forum for discussion of matters of interest to the gift industry, the Gift Association of America focuses on improving services to the general public and on the success of the industry.

MICHIGAN RETAILERS ASSOCIATION
www.retailers.com

Michigan Retailers Association offers retailers merchant business services including credit and debit bank card processing, worker compensation insurance, and legislative advocacy.

NATIONAL ASSOCIATION OF LIMITED EDITION DEALERS
www.naled.com

This organization is designed for retailers of collectibles and limited edition merchandise including the finest figurines, Christmas ornaments, dolls, plates, crystal, prints, houses, plush, miniatures, and musicals.

RETAIL CONFECTIONERS ASSOCIATION OF PHILADELPHIA, INC
phillycandyshow.com

This group was founded in 1918 for the purpose of sharing information and knowledge about candymaking and retailing among the Philadelphia area confectioners. Over the years, the local focus has expanded, and the RCAP currently has over 300 active and associate members throughout the United States and Canada. Today these candymakers and suppliers still share information to maintain very high quality chocolate and hard candy.

AWARDS AND RECOGNITION ASSOCIATION
www.ara.org

Focusing on the awards, engraving, and personalization professional, ARA features a monthly magazine, trade shows, education, and more.

20

If It's Not One Thing...

Here's a term I really hate: networking. I am still trying to find a terrific synonym for it because I love the concept. We all know that other retailers have the answers, but how do you find them when you have questions? At shows I always talk to everybody in line for the ladies' room or while I wait for food at the concessions. I've learned a lot from them and had many questions answered, but sometimes I need information when I don't have to go to the bathroom. What then?

Seminars are always attended by people who are happy to share information, sources, and ideas. Linda and John Wolbert own Sign of the Dolphin in Madeira Beach, Florida. The delightful John sent this:

Dear Mary Liz:

It was a great pleasure to meet you in High Point. The Dolphin must develop a true web store, but the 'how' is going to be the trick.

Aside from the web store, one of my long-standing and unfulfilled goals is to set up a group of about six or eight sharp retailers from various parts of the country, running similar stores in the same industry, for the purpose of sharing and comparing problems and basic infrastructure needs. Such as banking, merchant services, phone services, insurance, freight and parcel services, personnel management and benefits, advertising, and so on. I was once aware of groups of this type in the jewelry industry where store owners would meet every 60 days to compare notes and help each other. Because they were all in different cities, it worked well for all. At least they are all still doing well.

There may be a group of specialty retailers in this country doing this networking concept, but I am not aware of it. This is not intended to get any personal business data that is highly confidential such as sales volumes, profits, and things independent retailers protect. The general subjects that we all experience daily are the topics I want to know about.

Best regards, John Wolbert

Ryp Walters at OverCoffee Productions thinks John is correct, too. OverCoffee designed design and hosts our website, which will is a forum for all things retail.

"Retailers will be able to share their experiences with others," Ryp notes. "Whether it's tips on how to survive trade shows, marketing and promo ideas, new ways to display products ... whatever topics the users want to explore."

The site will feature easy-to-navigate areas that offer topics geared for a retailer's level of experience in the industry. As the site grows, it will provide opportu-

Wolbert's top ten

Here are the questions John Wolbert proposed to get us going

1. Insurance needs. How much is enough? Should we buy business interruption coverage? How much liability coverage? Which companies have the best coverage and rates?

2. Banking. Can you find a bank that will waive service charges? What fees can be negotiated? Is a local bank more flexible than a national bank? Which one?

3. Computers and POS systems. How can you convince older workers to try the new system? Is the warehouse capable of creating barcode pricing tags or must the buyer do it all?

4. Manpower. Where do we find good workers? (Steal them from competitors?).

5. Determining wage ranges. Acceptable percentage of labor costs to gross revenues?

6. Employee benefits. Time off requests and how to be fair.

7. Appropriate dress code.

8. Advertising and promotion. What works best? What percent of sales is too little, or too much?

9. Shipping and Receiving. Incoming controls and outgoing costs. UPS or FedEx? Time to review or change? Has US Postal Service become more competitive?

10. Security and Safety issues. Cameras and alarms, phone systems, recording equipment.

It's Another meeting

It's Another may be coming to a show near you! Check our website (itsanother.org) for the dates of upcoming events. We generally have two or three meetings per show season.

nities for private or restricted forums run by registered users, and much more. Areas for retailers with brick-and-mortar operations will be differentiated from those who sell online only.

So after all this excitement, what to call this fledgling organization? John Saxtan had a great idea: The Black Ink Society … keeping retailers out of the red. I like it, but we have issues in addition to money. I kept searching, trying to find just the right name. I thought about whether I could write a column about naming a business. After all, in retail, if it's not one thing, it's another.

Then it hit. Eureka! The name is: It's Another. Visit our website, www.itsanother.org, come to a meeting, send us your questions, share your best ideas, and make new friends. It's not networking; it's another thing entirely.

Running an independent retail store while also running a home and raising a family, which many of us do, is more complicated than anybody who is not in the business could ever imagine. As you know, if it's not one thing, It's Another.

21

It's Market Time!

After Christmas your store is probably back to normal, all vestiges of the holidays neatly packed away. Christmas is once again a memory, another retail season behind you.

Ho! Ho! Ho! Stop relaxing. It is time to start again and begin planning for the next Christmas season, which is just around the bend.

My mother, Bert Curtin, had a Christmas store in Santa Barbara for many years. I recall her saying, "The best time to place my Christmas orders was in January while I still remembered exactly what happened and how long the after-Christmas sale lasted. If I waited until summer to order. I started to think everything was cute again, and I'd order too much, even with the previous year's sales figures in hand."

Her point is well taken—begin planning your fourth-quarter purchases at the beginning of the year, while the previous season is still clear in your mind.

The winter shows are a buyer's delight. There are more show specials, closeout merchandise, and dating programs than ever—giving you lots of opportunities to increase your margins with discounts, deals on freight, and other incentives. January is a good time to visit a new market or extend your usual buying trips.

Many retailers notice that when they attend different shows, they see merchandise that is entirely new to them—even though much of the same product is displayed at the shows they shop regularly.

Take a key employee

When you plan your next buying trip, consider taking an essential member of your staff, even if that person is not a buyer. It is a great way to make the employee feel important and respected, it brings a new set of eyes to the show and gives her a better connection to the merchandise.

Take only one person at a time. If you take several people it is much too distracting. The side benefit is that when you return she'll let the rest of the staff know that a trade show is not a vacation.

DATING PROGRAMS

Holiday dating programs are essential to both the manufacturers and the retailers. From the supply side, these early orders allow vendors to project their sales early enough to plan production, warehousing, and shipping. Since they ship the orders in August and September, they can use their warehouses more efficiently.

Retailers who order seasonal merchandise early in the year receive the goods early in the season, are assured of delivery of the hot items (many are sold out by the summer markets), and don't have to pay the bill for 60-120 days. In most cases dating orders are the first ones shipped when the merchandise is available, making you the first to have the newest goods. Your customers will learn to think of you first. What a great deal!

In addition, since the merchandise is in the stores early, items often sell through and can be reordered before the holiday rush (if stock is available), giving you extra turns.

Dating programs are usually offered to all customers, but credit is often tighter than usual due to the extended terms. If your payment history is less than exemplary you may have trouble qualifying.

There are often several tiers to these orders, with greater dollar amounts qualifying you for bigger discounts and better deals.

There are a few things to watch out for, however. Don't place a huge order just to get extended terms!

Sometimes the incentives are so attractive that it is very tempting to over-order and end up with too much merchandise and a big invoice due in December. Also, keep a good open order record so you are aware of what is coming. It's easy to forget what is on order when you work eight months in advance.

Undoubtedly the largest category for dating is holiday trim, so ask every vendor in this area about the programs they offer. As with any dating programs, be sure you learn all the rules and details so you can decide if the program really works for you before you commit. Think before you order!

Forget the reorders!

Trade shows are for new products, line and working face to face with manufacturers. Writing basic reorders at a trade show can waste time that would be better spent looking for new merchandise, attending seminars, networking or even going out to lunch.

SHOW SPECIALS

Ask every vendor what incentives he or she is offering. Look for: freight allowances on orders over a certain dollar amount, free displays, discounts for ordering at the show, special pricing on products, advertising allowances, and longer terms. Competition is fierce these days, and many manufacturers will work a little harder to get your business.

While you certainly don't want to choose a line just because of a great deal, many of your usual vendors have specials you shouldn't miss.

Retail success demands new products, exciting displays, and careful attention to the bottom line. You'll need every discount, freight allowance, and opportunity buy you can find. Your customers will be looking for bargains as well as consistent good merchandising. Go to the shows! Find the deals! While you are there, have a little fun, see a show, have a great dinner. Retailers deserve a break, too.

22
Make a List for the Market!

Each season as I prepare for the trade shows, I make a list of things to do at each show and goals to accomplish. I am certain that putting a goal on the list is the first step towards accomplishing that goal, however esoteric. As an example, the first item on my list for quite a while was "find a husband." Well, that worked successfully in 1989, and I am still married and checking off the goals on my list, one by one.

Here are the top four things to put on your lists for the show season.

BE PREPARED!

At year end, as you prepare your inventories and open-to-buy for the next year, stop and take time to think about your business. As well as the facts and figures you are accumulating, take into consideration the customer comments, the requests from your employees, and suggestions from the trade magazines.

Take a few quiet minutes to review your sales, especially in the fourth quarter. What sold and what didn't? Which displays or promotions worked? Which didn't? Where did you under-buy or over-assort? Which were your problem companies? Which were dependable suppliers?

Go through your store mentally, and try to recall the different departments and your impressions of their performance. This information will be invaluable as you plan your next year's inventory, and it will help you focus on tailoring this year's stock to your needs.

HAVE FUN AT THE TRADE SHOWS

After a long day at the show, don't spend every evening extending orders. This year, check the websites of the show you will be attending, and see what after-hours events they are offering. If nothing show-related appeals to you, look at the city's website and visit a museum, see a play, or at least try a new restaurant. By the way, a shop-till-you-drop evening in a trade mart doesn't count.

Make your evening out a priority, put it on your to-do list, and plan it before you leave home. Here are a few great evening ideas:

The New York International Gift Fair has two fabulous events. Did you know that the GLM theater event (Tuesday night of the gift show) is always a great bargain? GLM buys excellent orchestra seats for a top Broadway show and makes them available to buyers and exhibitors at less than box office prices!

Keep a List

Keep your old to-do lists for reference. It is not only fascinating to see what was on your agenda in past years, but it can act as a journal. You may even find that re-reading the lists will help you see the changes your business has gone through and the progress you have made. Occasionally, you may find something on an old to-do list that you have forgotten you should still be doing.

What a deal—a bargain for seats you can't even buy without a broker! Tickets sell out quickly. Visit www.glmshows.com for details.

The Dallas International Gift Show is home to the ARTS awards. For a glamorous evening out, consider attending this black-tie tribute to the leaders in the home decorative accessory industry. The ARTS Awards Gala is a tribute to the leaders in Home Furnishings and Decorative Accessories. Visit www. accessoriesresourceteam.org for information.

Key Vendor List

Do you have a list of your key vendors? These are the manufacturers who provide excellent customer service as well as product that consistently retails well and ships quickly. Always keep money in your open-to-buy for these companies—they will keep you in business as trendier products and resources come and go.

SEMINARS

Make it a point to go to at least one seminar at each gift show you attend. An attendee at one of my seminars said she always attends at least one presentation each market. "I usually get a lot of information and ideas at the seminars, but if I get just two good ideas out of a presentation, it is worth my time to listen." Seminars are a great place to meet people, too. They are inexpensive or even free, interesting, and you'll learn something from every one.

FIND THREE LINES WITH BETTER THAN KEYSTONE MARKUPS

This should always be on your list of things to buy. Keep those high margins a priority! Whether you find new lines or add new merchandise from existing vendors, there are there are lots of products with long marks.

Now, start your own list and have a great time at market!

23

How I Spent My Summer Vacation

One night, as I was packing for yet another trade show, my daughter asked, "Are all of the shows you go to the same, Mom?" She made me start thinking about what, exactly, is the point of going to more than just one show, preferably the closest one. After all, isn't the merchandise pretty much the same everywhere? Isn't one very much like another?

Well, shows aren't the same everyplace. While the big players are certainly at almost every one, each trade show has a few lines that show in only one place, new presentations for the products you have seen elsewhere and may already carry, and educational programs unique to the market. Plus, it is exciting to go someplace new and see what treasures you may find. It's not all about size, either. The Philadelphia Gift Show is a smaller, regional market where I recently discovered two excellent lines that I had overlooked at bigger markets.

Trade shows are more than handy places to write orders. They are educational opportunities as well. Here is what I brought home from the shows:

BUY WITH A PLAN

This is, flat out, the most important thing I can share with you. Don't just shop for items! As you buy, think about how the merchandise will look in your store. Plan the display, think about the props you may need, and what other products will work with it. If you have no idea where an item will go on your display shelves, *don't buy it!*

As a retail example, look at Crate & Barrel or Pottery Barn. They show coordinated merchandise from numerous vendors to carry out their current themes.

Two's Company always has fabulous displays in their showrooms and temporary booths. The merchandise looks like a million bucks and makes you want to buy, buy, buy. This is what you want your customers to feel when they walk into your store, right? Well, notice this about Two's Company presentations: everything is organized by collection. The showrooms and booths are broken into rooms, each with a specific theme, tied together by product mix and color. Think of themes and collections when you are buying for your store. Tell your customers a story with your assortments … make it your mission to buy enough related merchandise to have a terrific display. Think about where it will go in your store, what you will merchandise with it, and how everything will synergize.

Your plan for presentation is as important as your open-to-buy. It is very easy to buy a little of this, some of that, one of those and end up with a store

Reverse Shopping

When you walk a show or trade building, try starting in a new place each market so you get a fresh perspective. Try to walk the aisles twice, especially in the sections that are very important to your store, once in each direction, to be sure you have missed nothing. Walk through new parts of the show, too. You may find a treasure where you least expect it.

that resembles a garage sale. Of course, if you really work on it, you could make Garage Sale a theme ... but only if you are doing it intentionally.

Buy enough

A puny display will not sell merchandise. If you are hesitant about a line, you are often better off passing on the order altogether than "trying just a little to see if it sells". Even the fastest selling, hottest items will slow when the inventory starts to look thin and picked-over Make a statement!

HIT THE MALLS

Most of us never have time to shop around at home. Take an evening or an afternoon while you are away to shop other stores, preferably with another retailer so you can talk about what you see. Shop for ideas! Look at motifs, colors, themes. Make notes (inconspicuously) of merchandise ideas as well as presentation. To find the exciting stores in any city, ask the reps at the show or take one of the retail tours offered at many shows.

LOOK AT DISPLAYS, NOT JUST PRODUCTS

Whether you are at market or the mall, take time to look at the presentations of everything. Walk through and just look at the displays, colors, and presentations, whether they relate to your product mix or not. See how the professionals show product. You will almost always find a few ideas to rework for your store.

DIP INTO THE MAGAZINE BINS

There are bins brimming with trade magazines at every show. They are free and a great way to try a new magazine. Even the periodicals that don't directly apply to your business may have a tip or two worth remembering. Take one of each!

24
Amazing India

February 25, 2004. 6:00pm, Eastern Standard Time.

I take off from Detroit to Amsterdam, en route to the Indian Handicrafts and Gifts Fair, held in New Delhi. After two eight-hour flights and two hours in Amsterdam, I land at 1:30 in the morning Delhi time, on the other side of the globe, in another world. The cab ride to the hotel is amazing! Traffic even in the middle of the night is wild with vehicles driving all over the road. In the cab the next morning, I see horses, camels, and an elephant in the streets of New Delhi, sharing the road with rickshaws, trucks, and the occasional wandering cow.

Isn't this what we always hoped a buying trip would sound like? Everybody knows that trade shows are vital to a retailer's existence. Wholesale markets are where we find the newest products, scout for trends, find merchandising ideas, and see great displays. Visiting a new trade show is always an eye opener—even familiar product often looks different when displayed by other hands. I still get excited walking in the door to a new show, sure that this is the market where I will spot a real winner or see a booth that will knock my socks off. Whether it is a major market, a tiny regional show, or a market in a new industry, there is always the possibility of something great waiting to be discovered.

The Indian Handicrafts and Gifts Fair provided all this and more. The booths were terrific, the products were fascinating, and the venue was exotic. You just don't see snake charmers on the street in Atlanta or camels on the way to the Javits Center. Now, I realize that New Delhi is not on the regular trade show circuit for most American buyers, but it is certainly worth a visit. The fair is organized by India's Export Council for the Promotion of Handicrafts, under the aegis of the Ministry of Textiles. Their mission is to bring the entire range of handicrafts and gifts available in India to the world. The booths are stunning, and the halls are easy to work. Surprisingly, communication is no problem as English is widely spoken.

India is a major resource for our market, supplying a diverse selection of products, including textiles, portable lighting, furniture, brass, decorative accessories, accent furniture, tabletop, paper products, stationery, jewelry and accessories, scarves, ready-to-wear, and glass, as well as traditional hand-made Indian crafts. These artisans are capable of making anything the buyer needs. India is a rapidly growing resource for the gift and home industries in the United States and across the world, offering excellent prices and superior workmanship. This is a country full of entrepreneurs, eager to please their foreign customers.

The VIIth World Bamboo Congress was held in conjunction with the fair. "Bamboo for development—Poverty Alleviation & Employment Generation" was the theme. Bamboo is a natural product, of course, and not only renewable,

Interesting fact

There are more English-speaking people in India than there are in the United States.

69

India Expo Centre
& Mart

Buying in India is even easier now. This state-of-the-art building houses over 2 million square feet of exhibition space in addition to 400 showrooms. Open year-round, the India Expo Centre and Mart, the products shown include home décor, jewelry, gifts, furniture and handicrafts.

"The purpose behind the India Expo Centre and Mart is to bring the world to India, and to bring Indian products to the world," says Kevin Stephens, managing director of Saffaire Consultancy Services, which was hired to help build awareness of the Centre with U.S. retailers. "Every aspect of the Center and its markets is being devised to make it easy, efficient, and cost-effective for buyers to travel to India and see the full scope of gifts, textiles, and decorative furnishings across the board, all under one roof."

The concept for India Expo Centre grew out of the activities of the Export Promotion Council for Handicrafts (EPCH), a division of the Indian government's Ministry of Textiles. EPCH coordinates and promotes the export of handicrafts from India, and also organizes trade shows including the Indian Handicrafts & Gift Fair, as well as buyer-seller meetings, conferences, and study tours to keep Indian exporters abreast of the latest trends in the markets worldwide.

but virtually unstoppable. Increasing the marketability of bamboo in a number of commercial and industrial applications will help to reduce poverty in some of the neediest areas of India. The uses showcased in this pavilion were astounding, from homes built of bamboo to decorative accessories.

There were several craftsmen demonstrating their skills in the Bamboo Pavilion. One of my favorite sights of the trip was watching a man, seated on the floor, engaged in the ancient art of carving sandalwood, while talking on his cell phone.

When I went to India, my plan was to find unbelievable products at fabulous prices that an independent store could import directly to achieve stellar margins, thereby paying for their trip and a great deal of personal shopping. My goal was to give you completely rational, fiscally sound reasons to attend this fabulous market. The reality about import is far different, although the personal shopping was exceptional.

The Indian fair is really targeted to chain stores, wholesalers, and distributors. Buyers from many of the lines you carry in your store shop this show for resources. They can order stock items or develop custom products with the vendors at the fair. For the independent retailer, importing product from Asia it is not just a matter of ordering large quantities and waiting a little longer for your merchandise. There are infinite details and many possible complications. From quality issues to monsoons, there is a host of problems waiting for the hapless shipment. I have a new level of respect for importers and their agents.

However, there are still excellent reasons to consider a trip to a major international show like the Indian Handicrafts and Gifts Fair. You will see the sources for many of the products you now carry—and you'll have a chance to see the hands that create the hand-made product. This is a trip you will never forget—and it will translate into increased energy and inspiration for your business.

The cost of a trip is surprisingly affordable. Hotel show rates range from $50.00 to $160.00 per night and meals are very reasonable. Airfare is the biggest expense, but tickets are available starting around $1,300 roundtrip.

The Indians are unbelievable hosts, generous and thoughtful. Visitors are revered in India, so touring here is a delight. Almost everyone speaks English to some degree, and strangers as well as business associates are accommodating and unfailingly gracious.

In addition to Delhi, I visited two other cities: Jaipur, the Pink City, where I visited the furniture factory and showroom of Alps Corporation, and Agra, the home of the Taj Mahal, which is beyond belief. Everything you have heard about it is true—and more. My visit was particularly romantic. I was traveling with Carla Webb, senior editor Tabletop at HFN and her significant other, Paul O'Connor. To the delight of our guide, several strangers, and Carla, Paul proposed to her while we were at the Taj Mahal, and she accepted. Appropriately, the Taj Mahal is the monument of a man's love for a woman. The countryside is beautiful, and the historical sites are fabulous, but I found watching the people going about their daily business to be most fascinating. A family of four perched on a single motor scooter darting through traffic is a common sight, as are women carrying jars of water on their heads, walking down the center of a four lane freeway. Seeing cows walking through a mall and camels in downtown streets amazed me. Visiting India and seeing the new world side by side with the old is astounding. I would go again in a heartbeat.

As the Penny Pinching Retailer, you may wonder why I am suggesting such an unusual trip when most of the product is available from a source at a gift show near you. I came home with a new awareness of the breadth of products from this magical country, astounded that I have actually seen a very few of the many people who make the merchandise we sell. I am thrilled with the colors I saw and have a new appreciation for elephants.

What is in India for you? Excitement, amazement, and a lot of great merchandise.

For more information about the Indian Handicrafts & Gifts show, visit the Export Promotion Council for Handicrafts at www.epch.com

The India Pavilion in Dallas Market Center is an 8,000 square foot showcase of Indian products, the first official permanent showroom of Indian merchandise in the United States Contact www.dallasmarketcenter.com for more information.

25
Country of Origin: Ireland

Let's just skip the leprechauns today. Also the shamrocks, shillelaghs, and step-dancers. Maybe even avoid discussing the color green entirely. I am as Irish as the next third-generation Irish American, and proud of it; but I was totally unaware of the variety of fine products my very distant Celtic cousins are producing until I was lucky enough to attend Showcase Ireland, the Irish craft, gift, fashion, and interiors fair. This fair is the home to great products in all categories, with an emphasis on handcrafted merchandise.

This trade show, Ireland's largest, attracts buyers from all around the globe who are interested in design, style, and craftsmanship. It also features the Source, a juried selection of crafts selected for quality and commercial ability, chosen by a panel of national and international buyers. Many of the companies have warehouses and distribution in the United States, others are familiar with shipping to the US, and a few are so new that they have never exported. All are interested in selling to the American market, and American customers have proven interest in their products.

The most exciting find for me was the great number of manufacturers combining traditional crafts and superior workmanship with contemporary design to produce products that are perfectly suited to today's consumer.

My new career

I was thrilled to attend Showcase Ireland. The absolute highlight of the trip, however, was my lesson in crystal cutting at Waterford, under the watchful and encouraging tutelage of master cutter John Stenson. The factory is unbelievable and seeing the craftsmen at work was inspiring, but the chance to cut crystal was unbelievable. While I was convinced it was the potential beginning of a new vocation, there was absolutely no assurance from anyone that I had a future in their factory. Regretfully, I turned in my Waterford lab coat and returned to my regular life.

TABLETOP

Irish crystal has been justly renowned for centuries. Beautifully faceted wineglasses, hand cut bowls, sparkling candlesticks … but have you seen the contemporary collections from many of the familiar names?

Tipperary Crystal (www.tipperarycrystal.com) has introduced the Gift Collection from Louise Kennedy, dramatic products that look like they came straight off the couture runway. Tipperary also has a grouping called Allsorts (named for the licorice candies) that features stripes and dots and is absolutely a knock-out.

Waterford (www.waterford.com) is certainly one of the most famous and popular names in crystal. I toured their plant, guided by the delightful John Connolly and Jim O'Leary. I was captivated by the enthusiasm of the people who work there and the gorgeous product, not to mention the replica of the Waterford ball that is dropped each year in Times Square. While I had felt previously that Waterford is expensive but worth the price, now that I have seen how it is made, I think it is almost a bargain. Visit www.waterfordvisitorcentre.com for information on the tour.

Waterford's W Collection, designed by John Connolly, is clean and simple, with modern lines and a very fresh appeal. It makes a lovely counterpoint to the traditional pieces, perennial best sellers.

Stephen Pearce Pottery (www.stephenpearce.com) has been producing earthenware goods in Shanagarry, Cork, since 1950, using organic local clay and 250-year-old techniques. Their dinnerware and accessories are designed for everyday use with a warm, natural feel that makes them a pleasure to hold and use.

Each of these companies also has a portable lighting category, and don't miss the fabulous chandeliers from Waterford and Tipperary.

JEWELRY

Naturally, to cover the show completely, I was honor-bound to visit the jewelry booths and be sure I missed nothing. Jewelry, along with all personal accessories, is one of the hot categories in the gift market. From classic designs to modern interpretations of the Trinity Knot, Celtic spirals, and the Claddagh, there are pieces for almost every type of store. You'll find sterling and gold, with and without stones, and price points at all levels.

Of particular note are the bridal collections. This is a very strong category in the US, as many Americans acknowledge their ancestry with these pieces for anniversaries, weddings, and special occasions—or no occasion at all, as I frequently remind my husband. Visit these sites: www.fadojewelry.com, www.tjh.ie, and www.thecatandthemoon.com to see for yourself.

PERSONAL CARE

Looking to infuse some new life in your personal care department? Fragrances of Ireland (www.perfume.ie) is the creator of a unique collection of Irish perfumes, colognes, soaps, and toiletries. Inis, the energy of the sea, is a unique scent that is light and appealing and comes in a beautiful bottle with a crystal top.

Ri Na Mara (www.rinamara.com) is a new line of Irish seaweed cosmetics that are quite appealing. The fragrance is delightful, and now that I have used the face cream, I am certain I look younger than I did just a week ago.

Fragrance Boutique (www.fragrance-boutique.com) has brought new life to citronella. Their Outdoor Living Collection features sage green citronella candles. (Yes, it is true. They are not yellow.) They are scented with lemongrass, presented in chic white ceramic bowls. They have a terrific baby collection, too.

Bog Standard (www.bogstandard.ie) offers a delightful small collection of Irish products, including linen tea towels, soaps, and candles. "Irish Winter" scented candles might be just the thing to put a little aroma in your store when the January blahs arrive.

TEXTILES

Sweaters! Throws! Hats! It is a cold winter afternoon's dream to feel these fabulous woven treasures.

West End Knitwear (www.sweaters.org) has manufactured traditional Aran products since 1957. They introduced a collection called NUA ("new" in Gaelic) which is young, modern, and luxurious.

John Hanly & Co (www.johnhanly.com) is a family run business that has been making scarves and throws since 1893. They are 100% Irish made and 100% fabulous: great colors, beautiful designs, and good value.

All of us in the gift business are always looking for new resources and fresh product. Showcase Ireland displays a diverse mix of merchandise from new resources as well as familiar vendors. It was inspiring to see hand crafted product with a fine pedigree of hundreds of years of tradition combined with modern sensibilities and a highly evolved sense of design. I was thrilled with the number of family run businesses and the sense of history.

Take a look at Irish product. It's not just for St. Patrick's Day.

SOURCES

Go to a foreign show

Even if you are not ready to import, a trade show in another country is inspiring and exciting. You may find products that you will buy from a domestic resource, but having seen them in their native land will give you a better understanding not only of the product but of the people who produce it.

ENTERPRISE IRELAND
www.enterprise-ireland.com

Enterprise Ireland is a trade organization dedicated to the development and promotion of Irish business in world markets. Contact them directly for more information about the show, sources, or anything else Irish. Ask for Maeve O'Malley, senior marketing executive or Ruairi Curtin, vice president.

THE NORTH AMERICAN CELTIC BUYERS ASSOCIATION
www.celticbuyers.com

NACBA is the trade association representing Celtic (Irish, Scottish, and Welsh) retail stores in the United States and Canada. Its mission is to facilitate communication among businesses, vendors, trade boards, and trade show organizers, and to develop programs of cooperative advertising, promotion, travel, buying, shipping, and education for its members.

The Celtic Marketplace Trade Show
www.celticshow.com

Sponsored by the NACBA, this show focuses on St. Patrick's Day and Christmas merchandise. Target buyers are Celtic stores. It is held in Lombard, Illinois, each September.

Showcase Ireland
www.showcaseireland.com

Ireland's premier craft, gift, fashion, jewelry, and interiors fair. When you visit Showcase Ireland, you join buyers from over 30 countries worldwide to see exclusive contemporary and classic merchandise from 600 exhibitors.

26

Paper Money: Where the Profits Are in the Stationery Business

Stationery is one of the most exciting and innovative categories in the gift business. Because paper is such a responsive and relatively inexpensive medium, it is easy for designers to follow trends and refresh their lines often. There are crafters, stampers, and scrapbookers looking for lots of parts and pieces. These customers love classes that give them lots of new ideas. Then there are card buyers who are always shopping for something fun. Don't forget the letter writers who need beautiful paper and notecards.

I am a huge fan of the National Stationery Show. There are always loads of brand new companies making their debuts at the show, established manufacturers introducing new merchandise, and many companies showcasing their lines in company booths. There are great displays, opportunities to see the latest trends and colors in the gift industry, and the chance to meet the top people from your favorite companies. Trends change very quickly, and you'll see them here first. The fact that it is held in New York in May, the prettiest month of the year, is an added bonus.

GREETING CARDS

Cards are the backbone of the stationery business, and there are lots of great companies with interesting and creative lines on the market. With the baseline retail now at $2.25 per card (and price points of $5.95 and higher for special occasion cards), this is an important category. Everybody sells cards now ... grocery stores, car washes, hardware stores ... even pet shops. These "one rack retailers," however, are really just conveniences for shoppers and do not seem to have an adverse effect on traditional card shops. To become a destination for card shoppers, a store needs an interesting and varied card selection that changes frequently.

As you choose the vendors you will carry, consider margins as well as your assortment. To maximize your returns with any of the larger manufacturers, think in terms of running feet. With a commitment of eight or twelve feet in one line, you will qualify for discounts, free freight, fixtures, and return privileges. The larger display of a line will also increase sales due to the strong presence from that company. Work with your salespeople to find the correct presentation for your store from each company you are considering. You will want to consider your location and the demographics of your customer base.

A note on greeting cards

35 percent of gift and stationery retailers are planning to add greeting cards to their store's merchandise mix, according to a recent survey sponsored by greetings, etc. magazine. Some 28 percent responding to the survey also plan to add boxed notecards to their mix. Why? Greeting cards draw customers.

Offering a good selection of greeting cards is a customer service. You're saving your customer the effort of going somewhere else to buy a card for his gift purchase. Greeting cards are also impulse purchases, helping to add dollars to the store's bottom line. Having unique cards that customers can't get elsewhere can make your store a destination for card aficionados (yes, they're out there). Cards with great verses get customers to linger in the store longer, too.

Greeting cards are not high-ticket items, so they're a relatively safe investment. Choose the lines that are right for your clientele, keep the displays fresh, and enjoy the profits!

—Kathy Krassner
editor-in-chief
greetings, etc. magazine

Avanti, Blue Mountain, Shade Tree, Portal Publications, Marcel Schurman, Oatmeal, and Renaissance all have excellent programs dedicated to helping the retailer sell more product and increase their profits per square foot. You can look for as much as a 10% discount on all products, free freight, free fixtures, and 100% return privileges with a large commitment. Choose the key lines for your store carefully, and be sure that you work closely with your salesperson to stay current with all new programs and products.

Seasonal cards are an important category: check out the new Auto Avanti program for an all-year, 24-pocket program of holiday cards. Auto Avanti customers receive product automatically, with 100% exchange privileges.

As well as the staple lines that are dependable and profitable, always keep an eye out for the new lines that have exciting and trendy product that keep your store looking fresh and your customer coming back frequently to see what's new.

STICKERS

Mrs. Grossman's Paper Company gave us the category of stickers 20 years ago … and has always provided phenomenal margins. Stickers on the roll are more profitable than those in the package. The basic 2"×2" paper stickers cost only 4 cents and retail for 15 to 25 cents … which is a very pleasant markup. The margins on other sizes and styles vary, but all exceed keystone. This line also offers everything your customers need for sticker crafting, from idea books to albums. Stickers are a staple category, actually selling to adults more than children for making scrapbooks, greeting cards, invitations, and stationery. Check out Mrs. Grossman's Red Heart program for even greater profits.

BULK PAPER

The Paper Company is an outstanding source for paper, cards, and envelopes in a variety of sizes and an enormous range of colors, including translucents, at mark-ups of 53% to 70%. Their fixturing is efficient, good looking, and completely offset. By the way, The Paper Company is now UPC coding their translucent papers and social notecards.

PAPER TABLEWARE

This is a category that requires a large assortment to be successful; and if you have to carry a lot of inventory in anything, you always want to buy it right. Boston International has over 200 styles, from florals to contemporary, traditional to museum reproductions.

DIE CUTTING MACHINES

Paper crafting continues to be a growing category in the stationery business. Handmade cards and invitations, scrapbooks, rubber stamp projects, and even quilters all use die cuts.

National Stationery
Show

*I have attended and loved the
National Stationery Show since
most of the cards were printed
on papyrus, scribes wrote the
verses and it was held in the
New York Coliseum. After
all these years, it is still one of
my very favorite trade shows.*

While there are lots of excellent ready-made paper die cuts available, making your own shapes is an extremely high-margin business. Ellison Designs and Accu-Cut Systems both offer fantastic die cutting machines and large assortments of dies, as well as first class customer support for their programs. While the initial investment for the machine and dies is a little hefty, it is well worth considering. Your sales of bulk paper (a high margin item) will increase dramatically, and your store will become a destination for crafters of all kinds.

Stationery is a category that turns quickly, has good (sometimes really good) margins, and is not terribly expensive. A superior card department is also a traffic builder. Customers come back frequently to see what's new as well as to buy for specific occasions.

Planning a card shop, complete stationery department, or even just a paper section in a store is easy and fun. Making that square footage more profitable is not difficult and well worth the time. Don't just ask "what's new?" Ask "what makes you the most money?" By the way, real money is closer than you might think at the Stationery Show. Did you know that Crane makes the paper the mint uses for currency?

IV

❦

Money Matters

27
Penny Pinching—Making Your Dollars Work for Your Store

Running a profitable independent retail store in the twenty-first century is more of a challenge than ever … and the challenge becomes even greater when spending slows.

So what is the poor, beleaguered retailer to do?

Think cheap. Increase your margins and decrease your expenses. More than ever, you must watch the bottom line and make sure you keep as much of every dollar sold as you possibly can. While profitability has always been important, when business takes a downturn it becomes crucial to have a healthy net profit.

Here are some money-saving ideas and strategies, sources for good buys, and tips from retailers. The goal is to have the money available to spend when and where you need it. You'll make that goal by cutting out the waste and by working to increase your gross profit margin on as many items as you can.

This does not mean spending your days reusing tin foil, sleeping in a roach motel at trade shows, or never taking your staff out to eat again. It does not mean cutting payroll. It also does not mean trying to bludgeon every manufacturer for discounts, freight, or special deals. It means finding the places you can save money without making your life (or anyone else's) miserable, learning to buy for maximum profit, and managing your cash flow intelligently.

When people are not shopping as much as they did, they are still shopping. Major chains as well as the Internet have made business harder every year for the independent retailer. The big box stores are expanding rapidly and opening new stores everywhere, selling many of the product categories independent retailers used to call their own. Even stores like Target and Kmart are encroaching upon our dollars as their selections improve and their product mixes become more varied and better designed.

As an independent retailer, you must provide what these stores cannot: more interesting and varied products, great service, imaginative and constantly changing displays, and a warm and pleasant atmosphere in the store. And you have to do it on a budget.

The first column

This was the very first column Penny Pinching Retailer column and I still believe every word I wrote. The money you save by running tighter business goes right to the bottom line … and into your pocket.

Show and Sell

Show your customers how to use the products you sell. While people are sometimes very imaginative, it is hard for them to visualize what your merchandise can do for them. If you sell vases or containers, show some filled with flowers or fruit. If you are in the craft business, be sure to have lots of examples of completed projects of all levels of difficulty.

SAVE MONEY ON SHIPPING

Freight is one of the biggest costs in retail, making it a terrific category to begin looking for savings. It is very expensive to move merchandise around the country, but with a little attention you can make some big savings.

"It's smart to be thrifty" (Macy's)

"Nobody undersells Gimbels" (Gimbels)

Bernice Fitz-Gibbon, wrote the slogan for Macy's and then Gimbel's stole her and she wrote their famous tag line. A pioneer in advertising and marketing, Fitz-Gibbon also introduced the "events" we find common these days: fashion shows, dance instruction, lectures, demonstrations.

1. Keep a freight log, listing the amount of freight, number of cartons, and type of merchandise on each order. This is a good record of your receivings in case of dispute with the company as well as an internal log.

2. Always count the cartons and check for damages before the delivery person leaves!

3. Check the invoice date against the receiving date to be sure that the invoice does not pre-date the shipment. Many stores pay 30 days after receipt of goods, as invoice dates vary widely from shipment dates.

4. Be certain you are not being over-charged for shipping. Occasionally, weigh each carton and check the freight costs against a current rate chart from the carrier. Smaller manufacturers frequently add a few dollars to the UPS cost for handling without notifying the customer. Don't pay it! If you have been overcharged, deduct the difference when you pay the bill.

5. Beware of small orders! Often the freight is such a high percentage of the invoice amount that the order becomes unprofitable at retail.

6. Tell your vendors to cancel small backorders. If the invoice total is less than $50.00, it is too small to receive (unless it's a special order for a customer, of course). Note to manufacturers: if you can afford to pay the shipping on these little orders, many customers will accept them.

7. Freight allowances are terrific. Quite often it is worth adding to your order (or waiting until you need a bigger order) to get the free or discounted freight. Don't get excited and over order just to get free freight, though. Always note freight allowances (or any special terms) on your purchase order. Sometimes the manufacturer cannot ship an order complete, causing the invoice to be below the free freight amount. If you met the minimum with your order, you are entitled to the freight allowance. Notify the vendor and deduct it from the invoice. Don't forget—the backorders are free freight, too.

8. Learn your freight classifications when shipping common carrier. If you carry merchandise that is large enough or in large enough quantity to ship by truck, be certain that your vendor is shipping it at the correct freight classification. This can mean a difference of hundreds of dollars on a single order.

9. When placing an order for furniture or other bulky and/or heavy merchandise, confirm the shipping arrangements with the manufacturer or rep. This is especially true with newer vendors, some of whom do not know all the ins and outs of shipping.

10. Review the retails on high-freight items. You may need to increase the selling price to recover your shipping costs.

If you implement just one money-saving tip, your bottom line will benefit. If you start to think really cheap, it can save your store.

SPEND WHAT YOU SAVE

When business is slow, DON'T STOP BUYING! If your customers didn't buy it last week, they probably won't buy it this week. Your customers still want new and exciting products, interesting displays, and a sense that your store is always changing and fun. When you have fewer customers, you have to provide a bigger selection to increase your chances of having something for everyone. Go to the shows and search for new vendors, look for merchandising ideas, and talk to your top suppliers about the best ways to sell their products. Move everything in the store around so the old stuff looks new.

28
Five Goals for Next Year

The end of the year in retail is really a big project. There are financial reports to run, inventory to count, merchandise to close out, buying trips to plan, and stores to re-merchandise. It's also the time to think about the coming year and how to improve your business. And, if you are an independent retailer, you have to do most of it personally (or at least supervise it closely).

But first, give yourself credit. If, like many of my readers, you are an owner-operator, you are vital to our nation's economy. You've stayed in business in the face of national economic down-turn, increasing competition from big box stores, and costs that constantly rise on every front. Like most mom and pop operations, you are working as a buyer, financial analyst, merchandiser, stock clerk, bookkeeper, human resource manager, I.T. specialist, and janitor (note: my husband, a long time independent retailer, had business cards printed with his name and the title "Head Window Washer"). Congratulations! You deserve to be proud of your business.

The "mom and pop" stores are the ones who set the trends, respond quickly to new items, and are the foundation of the gift industry. These are the stores that have distinct identities and reflect the passion their owners have for great product, wonderful display, and excellent customer service. Our industry would be nowhere without the moms and pops.

So, here are five suggestions to help you keep more of the money you make, run a better business and give back to your community.

SAVE MONEY

As you are doing your year-end financial work, don't forget to run a comparison report (between this year and last) on your expenses as well as your sales. Check utilities, professional services, freight, and supplies in particular, as these are areas where it is very easy for costs to creep up. You may be able to find significant savings in your costs which will immediately improve your bottom line. After all, saving the money you make is as important a goal as making more of it.

INCREASE YOUR MARGINS

Are you buying well? Don't forget to ask every rep and manufacturer for freight allowances, special purchases, opportunity buys, and other margin-enhancing

Recently I was in Santa Barbara, chatting with the very talented Marge Ellis, who owned a terrific store called Patchworks. Marge's shop was a delight: for 18 years she specialized in hand-crafted items, many from local artists, and supplemented her inventory with merchandise from of a number of well known vendors. As we were talking about business, she said "I was too cheap. I probably could have made a lot more money if I had bought more expensive things. They always sold".

Marge has an excellent point: it is very easy to underestimate what your customer will spend. Have price points for everyone, but always have some thing for the big spender. In addition, people who want the expensive piece but cannot afford it will often "buy down" to a less expensive item. In that case, the big piece helped sell the small one.

offers. Analyze your profit margins by department, category, or vendor to see what merchandise makes you the most money.

GET MORE PUBLICITY

Are you sending press releases to the newspapers, magazines, radio and television stations in your area? If not, it is time to build your press list and start sending information about events or classes in your store, new lines, or items you are carrying, sales and promotions, and anything else that is happening in your store. The shopping editors are dying for the information—and the resulting press is invaluable.

IMPROVE YOUR STAFF TRAINING

Your employees are absolutely crucial to your success (as well as your sanity). The better educated they are about your store policies and the merchandise you sell, the better job they will do. Do you have staff meetings to keep everybody up-to-date on the store news? A brief weekly get-together can keep them informed about new products, inventory issues, and in-store promotions.

Many reps are delighted to come to the store to teach the staff about their merchandise. Ask companies for samples of any consumable product to give your staff—once they've tried the goods they'll sell more.

OPEN YOUR VIRTUAL STORE

Do you have a website? If not, this is the year to build one. The number of people turning to the computer for everything from phone number look-up to shopping is increasing hourly, and your shop should be there. Even if you start with a simple web page that has directions to your store and basic information about your business, your customers will find it and find you. By the way, when you launch your site, contact your key vendors. Many companies will be happy to provide links to your site from theirs, bringing you new customers.

If you aren't selling on the web, it is time to look into it. Many independent retailers are finding that their web businesses are tremendous boosts to their bottom lines. Start by searching the web for the products you sell in the store to see who is selling similar merchandise and how it is priced. You'll get a good idea of the possibilities for the merchandise you sell.

eBay is another excellent way to sell on the web. Try eBay auctions and perhaps an eBay store for a quick, inexpensive, and easy way to begin selling on the web. See Chapter 31 for more tips on effectively using eBay for your business.

Personal Goals

It's not just about the store! Set some goals for yourself that will make your life easier, happier and better. Whether it is something simple like taking a walk every night after dinner or something more arcane like learn the shell game, think about what you need as well as what the business requires. Approach big things in small steps and give yourself credit for making the steps.

By the way, if you want to learn the shell game—a handy and potentially profitable skill—the place to go is www.threeshellgame.com.

Service first

The store that sells its wares for less but pays little attention to the service it renders does not meet with the success of the store with courteous employees. The public is not greatly interested in saving a little money on a purchase at the expense of service.

—James Cash Penney
Founder
JC Penney

Okay, there are five money-making goals for next year. Here's one more goal: do something good for somebody next year. Host a benefit event in the store, design a window that promotes a charity, donate merchandise to a local cause … your community needs you! In addition to helping others, you'll make new friends and friends turn into customers.

29

Build a Business Plan
Part One: Tell Your Story

Most of us with small businesses don't see the reason for a business plan. The vast majority of stores fly by the hems of their skirts or the seats of their pants. After all, we don't have boards of directors or investors breathing down our backs, so what's the point? Did you know that independent retail stores fail at a rate second only to restaurants? Maybe a business plan is a good idea after all.

Plans are nothing; planning is everything.

—Dwight D. Eisenhower

Although my husband (he prefers not to be identified, so we just refer to him as Steve) operated successful retail stores for 28 years, he did so without a formal business plan. With our new store it was time to get professional, so we wrote our plan. Now that we have done it (and not without more than a few cross words, let me add), I am a convert. You probably wouldn't build a house without blueprints, make a dress without a pattern, or drive cross-country without a map, would you? Your business deserves no less, whether it is a start-up or an established, successful enterprise.

If you are using your business plan to secure financing or attract investors, it must be comprehensive, well-written, and professional. If you are using it as an internal guide, itmay be very simple. Plans can range from just a few pages to hundreds. I hear that some initial business plans for famous companies were written on the backs of cocktail napkins. Any way you choose to approach it, let your personality, and that of your business, show. I guarantee that the exercise is worthwhile and you will garner valuable insights from the process.

We tend to think a business plan is all about money, but that is only half of it. Many companies have failed even though they had impeccable financing because their basic concept was flawed, their location was wrong, or they didn't understand their customer well enough.

EXECUTIVE SUMMARY

This title cracks me up, personally. Somehow, as a retailer, I never really feel like an executive, possibly due to the apron, dust, and broken fingernails. Anyway, this is the very first thing in most business plans; and it is the overview of what your business will be and why it will be successful. The executive summary will be much easier to write after you work on the next sections.

As you answer the questions below, don't skip over the hard ones or those that have distressing answers. Part of what you are doing here is finding the areas which need work.

TYPE OF BUSINESS

This is sometimes harder to answer than you might expect. What do you really sell? It is more than just the products you carry. If you are a craft or gourmet store, you may also be in the business of teaching classes. Think about what your customers will take away with them in addition to the merchandise. If you are a bookstore, will you also be a coffee house and bakery? Is your store going to be targeted to upscale or to budget-conscious consumers? If there is a store you are emulating, mention it and describe it.

PRODUCT MIX
(What do I sell and where will I get it?)

What are the categories, price points, and specific types of products in your store? Will you buy the merchandise from reps, local artists, and/or gift shows? Do you have key vendors? Do you know who offers the best margins?

CUSTOMER BASE
(Who shops here?)

Demographic Gaffe

As you profile your customer base, describe them by more than age and income. Include their interests, hobbies, attitudes and lifestyles. As baby boomers age but refuse to admit they are getting older, their interests often parallel those of consumers 20 to 30 years younger.

Think about who shops in your store. Consider the ages, income, educational levels, and occupations of your customers. When do they shop? How many kids do they have? Defining your customer well will help you plan your store, buy and merchandise your product better. Here is an example: Wal-Mart and Target are both mass merchants. One targets a fashion conscious consumer, the other is all about low prices. If you think about the customer base each wants, you will see how it impacts everything they do, from advertising to store design. The most basic bit of advice in sales: *know your customer.*

If you are already have a business, in addition to the customers you have, are there customers you are trying to attract? Who are they? What do you need to do to get them? Kmart was after the Target customer, so they added Martha Stewart and Joe Boxer products to infuse the style they were missing.

LOCATION

Where is your store? Why did you choose the spot? What is the customer count like? Are there neighboring businesses that help attract customers? Is parking adequate and where is it? If the location is less than ideal, you will need to think about how you can offset it.

COMPETITION

First, let me state that I believe in competition, and I think more retail in an area is good for everybody. However, I also believe in knowing what the competition is up to. Who is selling the same products? Is there anybody with a similar concept? Make a list of your main competitors, both large and small. Get out there and shop in them. By the time we had finished our business plan, my husband had visited every furniture store within 50 miles at least twice. When we began planning our initial buy for the store, we knew who had what and for how much, enabling us to avoid duplication and be aware of our price points.

Describe your competitors' businesses and include both their strong and weak points; then explain how you will compare and compete. You may want to include their store sizes and the lines they carry. Don't forget to shop mail-order catalogs and e-businesses.

MANAGEMENT TEAM

Who are you? Why are you opening this business, and what are your qualifications? This is essential information for financing or investors. For small businesses, it will help you understand what your strengths are and where you may need help. Go ahead, boast a little! List your experience and qualifications for all parts of the business. You know more than you think.

STAFF

Who will be there every day? How many people do you think you will need for the sales floor, stockroom, and office? What benefits can you give them? Describe your targeted employee as you do your customers. Remember that for many of our employees, the three most important perks are discounts, a pleasant work place, and flexible schedules. The thing that keeps your employees is appreciation, by the way.

If you already have a business, keeping a current plan for your business will help you stay on top of your competition, know who your customers are and what they want, and see how your business is changing.

If you are starting a business, writing the plan will help you see if the business you are proposing is viable, gauge whether it is likely to be successful, and map what you have to do to achieve that success.

Now, back to the executive summary. After working on the other sections, you should be able to describe your venture in a few sentences. How does it sound? Would you want to shop there? If it doesn't have the WOW factor, your idea needs more work.

The websites below will give you more ideas, advice, and guidance.

A FEW HANDY WEBSITES

PLANWARE
www.planware.org/bizplan.htm

ENTREPRENEUR MAGAZINE
www.entrepreneur.com/bizplan

INC. MAGAZINE
www.inc.com/guides/write_biz_plan

SMALL BUSINESS ADMINISTRATION
www.sba.gov/starting_business/planning/basic.html

BPLANS.COM
www.bplans.com/sp/businessplans.cfm

30
Build a Business Plan
Part Two: What About the Money?

Many of us open stores because we are passionate about product, design, or crafting. Some of us are in business because we had great ideas that we just had to share or saw a need in the marketplace that we could fill. Whatever the reason for beginning the business, if the finances are not managed properly, it will be very difficult to succeed, no matter how dynamic your concept. Managing and planning the funds in a small business is a huge challenge for many independent retailers. Heck, look at the big guys like Kmart or Restoration Hardware—it is challenging for everybody.

Previously we covered the beginning of the plan: describing your business, marketing plans, and the products you will carry. Now the harder part: planning your finances. If your business is new, you absolutely must look at the budgets and projections you will require. If you have an existing business, better planning and controls will make your cash go farther and help you plan for the inevitable problems every business faces. There are several great software programs that will help you build the financial base for your business and lots of websites that are full of information. Some are designed just for business planning and cover all facets of your plan, while others are bookkeeping software. Since "Steve" and I wrote our own business plan and did not depend on a package, we used the budgeting tools in QuickBooks, which will make it easy for us to compare the actual numbers to the projections when the store is up and running.

I did it and so can you

My husband (who still prefers to remain anonymous but truly does exist) and I opened a furniture, decorative accessory and gift store, called Leon & Lulu. We were forced to write a business plan to get the financing for the building and both of us have seen the benefits of the research, analysis and planning the plan requires. Even after writing a business plan together, and opening a store, our marriage remains intact.

BUDGET YOUR MONTHLY EXPENSES

Start with your fixed overhead costs. These, of course, are the numbers that do not change with market conditions and recur monthly. They include, but are not necessarily limited to: rent, utilities (including phone), property taxes, common area fees (and other expenses due the landlord in addition to rent), insurance (general insurance, workman's compensation, etc.), management (or permanent employee) salary/wages, benefits, and taxes, professional fees (accounting, legal, etc.), website maintenance, and so on.

Then make line items for variable expenses like advertising and promotion, freight, postage, bank and credit card charges, store supplies, travel to trade shows, bad debt, and an additional 3% to 5% of the total for miscellaneous and unexpected expenses.

Revisit and rewrite
your plan

*Once is not enough. Refer to
your plan every few months
and make adjustments as
the market and your busi-
ness change. Writing the plan
is an excellent start—using
the plan is when it will
really pay off for you.*

Purchases are ordinarily a large line item. Your purchases will vary month to month since you will need to buy more heavily in anticipation of strong selling times (Valentine's Day, Mother's Day, Christmas, and so on). Careful projections are essential. If you figure that 40% of your annual sales are in November and December, and the strong selling months will be 8% to 10%, then the rest will average around 3%.

Big tip: look for holiday dating programs, free freight, and return privileges to help you get through the cash crunch.

Bigger tip: pour as much of your profits as you can into adding inventory. Too much inventory is not ideal, but too little is usually fatal.

START-UP, OCCASIONAL, OR ONE-TIME EXPENSES:

Fixtures and lighting, building repair, signage, web design, new carpet, point-of-sale system ... while you can plan ahead for many of these items, build an emergency fund for surprises. Be sure you have the money or a line of credit available.

SALES PROJECTIONS

Now that we have an idea of what it will cost to run your business, let's talk about sales. You need an idea of what you will sell so you can purchase for it. If you have an established business, you can project your sales based on history, economic conditions in your area, and any changes to your store, like a new department.

If you are starting a new shop, sales projections are harder. First, research the average dollars per square foot for the type of business you are starting. You can find this information through trade organizations or online. For an independent general gift store, figure $80 to $150 per square foot. Second, think about the number of times you will turn your inventory per year. In the gift business, we figure two to four turns per year, depending on the product.

Calculate your sales based on the size of your shop. If you are opening a store that is 2,000 square feet, and you hope to sell $100 per square foot at retail, your volume will be about $200,000 per year. As a very general rule, smaller shops have higher volumes per square foot, so there is more room for adjustment. To achieve these sales figures, you will need an inventory valued at $50,000 wholesale and turn that inventory twice. I base this on a keystone (or double) markup, for mathematical ease. Gift stores, craft stores, florists, and so on all have different averages and turn rates, so do research for your specific type of store.

For your business plan, I suggest you take the low figures for planning purposes. It is never a problem to exceed your sales projections! Consider doing a spread sheet with different sales per foot numbers ($75-$100-$150). This will give you an idea if you can be solvent at the lower numbers as well as how profitable you would be at the higher numbers. As you build your history, always keep an eye on your turn rates. If your actual turn rate is too low, you may have too much inventory, and if it is too high your inventory may be too low (which is actually restricting higher sales).

It is difficult to predict many of these variables. Always, always, always estimate expenses on the high side and sales on the low side. Many new business owners are so excited about their new stores that they ignore some of the warning signs that may come up in their business plans. A good business plan will identify potential problems before all your time and dollars are spent. Entrepreneurs by nature are risk takers. Just be sure to look at your business plan numbers with a hard eye.

This is a synopsis of the absolute basics for a one-year, purely fundamental business plan. It is an important tool for running a profitable business and truly indispensable for a start-up. According to a study commissioned by AT&T, only 42% of small business owners make business plans ... but 69% of those who do make business plans say it is a major element of their success.

One more thing: as you are reviewing all this financial information, remember how important it is to keep your costs down and your margins up. Are there expenses you can cut or lower? Many businesses fail not because of a lack of capital or even due to slow sales, but because they used their money foolishly.

31

Been There, Bought That and Now You Wish You Hadn't

Here is a dilemma for those of us who hate to lose a nickel. Marking down merchandise seems all wrong to us. Shortening our margins is anathema. However, sometimes products, entire lines, or even whole departments just don't sell, and they have to go. Inventory that doesn't move ties up money and valuable floor space which should be used profitably on merchandise that sells.

Sometimes you will actually have to bite the bullet and mark things down … maybe even below what you paid for them. But before you do that, here are some ideas to help you get full retail, enabling those goods to leave your store and find their true homes elsewhere.

First of all, try to remember that at some point you actually liked the offending product and that you thought the product was viable when you bought it. I realize that after a few months in the store, slow movers seem to grow in size, to haunt you, and possibly even begin to emit an odor. Realize that there is always hope. Hiding or ignoring the dogs will not make them go away, anyway.

The Sale Customer

Get to know your sale customer: She is very important to your bottom line. Although marked down merchandise has terrible margins, the bargain hunters are the customers who help you get rid of slow moving inventory, giving you space in the stockroom and money in your open-to-buy. These customers are important to a well run business—market to them!

CLEAN IT UP

It is very tempting to ignore slow sellers and leave them in a dark corner where you can't see them too often. Pay attention to those barkers! Clean them up! Dust them, wash them, or polish them. If your merchandise looks dirty, dusty, and neglected, it will almost never sell, regardless of price.

MOVE IT AROUND

Re-merchandising your store is always a good idea generally, but for slow merchandise categories, change can be a lifesaver. An item that didn't work well (or at all) may have a better chance if you completely rethink the way you present it. The hardest problem is an entire line that doesn't sell. You may have to put it in several places before you find the right spot. Every time you move those dogs, try a different arrangement. Keep trying! Every time you re-merchandise, your store will look fresh and different, and at the very least, other things will sell due to the effort.

PAINT IT

Never forget what a friend you have in paint! Many pieces of furniture, frames, and other large objects can get a whole new look with a little paint and some imagination. You can also spray wreaths and floral arrangements. While you are thinking about paint, consider repainting some of your display pieces for a new look.

RE-PACKAGE IT

Many inexpensive items can be repackaged for a new look or to achieve a higher retail. Use clear cellophane bags, acetate boxes, baskets, and boxes. Consider adding ribbon (well tied) or your store label to the finished item. Whether you combine multiples of one item or a collection of related items, be sure your customers can easily see everything in the package. This works well for consumables like candy, candles, and soaps.

If you haven't discovered Amac boxes, call 800 852 7158 for a catalog. These clear plastic boxes come in lots of sizes and colors, are inexpensive, and fabulous. As well as protecting anything you place in them, they will add to the perceived value. A Beanie Baby found in a heap in a basket is an inexpensive piece of plush. The same Beanie Baby becomes an heirloom collectible when it is in an Amac box.

Conversely, some items will sell better out of the package. A novelty Christmas ornament in a cello bag is a cheap thing from China. Out of the bag, it is a hand-painted treasure.

ROMANCE IT

Try a new fixture, put it in the window, add descriptive signage, and find similar or complimentary merchandise to display with it. Make the product look important (after all, it is important to you to get rid of it). Use your wildest ideas! Fluff it up! Hang it from the ceiling! Try something silly—it just might work.

HIDE IT AND TRY AGAIN LATER

Sometimes, especially with an unusual piece, your customers will have seen it for so long they just don't see it any more. Put it in the back room for a few weeks, then bring it out and treat it like a new item. Sometimes you'll really get lucky, and the customer who has been considering it will come in frantically and ask what happened to it. When a slow seller finally moves, it seems somebody else always wants it the next day, for full price!

So, all of that didn't work. Now what? Your money is too valuable to hold on to slow moving merchandise, and your store will not look exciting when the merchandise does not change. No matter how cheap you are, sometimes you have to mark it down and *get rid of it*. This often happens with the last few pieces of a collection.

When you look at the stragglers of a successful product group, remember how much you sold at full retail. It helps keep your perspective, and you may even consider reordering rather than trying to dump the remains.

French Flea Market

You never know what treasures you'll find at a flea market. Exaclair, Inc, importer of terrific French stationery, has a selection of overstocks and discontinued items at fabulous prices in their Marche Aux Puce (that's "flea market" in French). These items are perfect to mark at regular retail for very high margins or to sell at promotional prices. To have your name added to the mailing list for the bi-monthly newsletter, email your informa- tion to info@exaclair.com To see the entire line visit the website at www.exaclair.com.

HAVE A SALE

Put those dogs in the storeroom and save them for a sale (a real sale, not just a constant markdown corner). If you have lots of odds and ends around the store, it can make your entire product mix look a little tired. If it doesn't sell and doesn't look good any more, hide it until sale time.

When you plan your sale, remember that a good sale is not just a vehicle to sell slow movers, but a money-making promotional event. Plan your sale care- fully. Look for promotional prices on merchandise and buy for the sale. Mark the items to their original retail, then discount them. With careful shopping, many of your sale items can still command a keystone mark up. Having some new and fresh products for the sale will give your merchandise mix a boost and make the older inventory look better.

Don't forget to promote your sale! Have a theme, a catchy name for the sale, and let your customers know the dates ahead of time so they will make a point of coming to your store.

Give your sale a firm beginning and end. When it is over, return the unsold merchandise to full price if it is still saleable product. If it is unsaleable, do not put it back on the shelves. It will neither sell nor make your store look good.

DONATE IT

After your sale is over, you will probably have a few pieces that still need to go. There are several ways to donate, some of which can generate terrific publicity for your store. Silent auctions or raffles are an excellent way to have your store name in front of many of your current as well as potential customers. This is a great use for interesting decorative accessories, pieces of jewelry, or a large gift basket.

One caveat for auctions and raffles: don't give them anything without think- ing of how it will look at their event. This is advertising for your store, and your donation should not look crummy or cheap compared to the others at the affair.

Mark your product well. Your logo, website, phone number, and address must be clearly visible, in letters large enough to read without glasses.

Does your overstock consist of lots of little things? Pediatric hospitals and schools always need and appreciate paper, pencils, stickers, craft items, and small toys. Charity resale shops will take almost anything, but be sure your store identification is off these items.

THROW IT OUT

This is an option when the item is filthy or seriously damaged. Just *get rid of it*. One more thing: try to figure out why the merchandise didn't sell so you can avoid the same mistake next time. Retail is a continuous learning experience. As you work to bring your customers new and exciting products, as a good buyer you are bound to have a few misfires. Go out and shop for new product! Take a few risks.

Better luck next time!

32
Many Happy Returns

What is worse than marking merchandise down? Returns. We all hope that merchandise will stay sold once it is out of the store, but the world is not a perfect place and things will come back. As merchants, our goal is to accommodate our customers without losing our shirts.

The problem has been exacerbated in the last few years by department, discount, and other chain stores adopting extremely liberal (one could even say ridiculous) return polices. These stores would take anything back, anytime, in any condition. They, in turn, would often just bounce the unsaleable merchandise back to the manufacturer for credit. An unlimited return policy is not a privilege the independent retailer enjoys, making it impossible to compete with the majors on this level.

In addition, the returns to vendors have cost manufacturers a fortune, especially since the stores who can make these returns are the stores buying at discounted prices and paying on extended terms. Their margins have suffered horribly from dealing with some of these accounts.

Fortunately, there is change in the air and many of the larger stores are seriously tightening up on their returns. Gone are the days of cash refunds without receipts ... often there is a time limit for returns even with the receipt, and many merchandise categories (like electronics and software) are often not returnable at all.

This is great news for smaller operations! The terms we can offer are now similar to the larger stores.

Accepting a return is your chance to satisfy your customer and help her find what she wants. Solving your customer's problem will make her loyal for life ... and she'll tell her friends. Of course, handling a return poorly is also a chance to get in a big fat fight, which can make an enemy ... and she will tell ALL of her friends.

The first step is to define a return policy, post it, and stick to it. The second step is to break your policy occasionally when it is appropriate. Nobody ever said retail was logical.

How does a thrifty merchant handle returns? You want to make your customer happy, but not affect your profits unduly. Keep your terms as simple as you can, so they are easy to understand and remember.

A reasonable policy is:

Full refund in 14 days with receipt (some stores give their customers up to 30 days)
All refunds must be in kind (credit the same form of tender used to buy the item)

Make it easy

When a customer returns something, she has money to spend. Make the return process as easy and efficient as you can, then help her spend her refund. With the right attitude, the money will never leave the store.

Store credit for returns after the refund period
No returns on special orders
Sale items are final sale
All merchandise must be returned in the condition it left the store

You may also consider exceptions for specific categories. For instance, no returns or refunds on comestibles, seasonal items, or formal wear.

STATE YOUR POLICY CLEARLY

Have clear, visible signs stating your return and exchange policies in the store as well as on your sales receipts. When you sell an item, restate the policy so there are no questions. Don't give your customer the chance to say, "I didn't know the policy!!! Nobody told me!!!" A few will say it anyway, but try to cover your bases.

FURNITURE AND DECORATIVE ACCESSORIES

Home is the hottest category in retail these days, and many merchants are selling furniture, portable lighting, decorative accessories, and wall art for the first time. This is merchandise that many people need to see in their homes before they can be sure it works, and thus it causes an inordinate percentage of returns. This is not necessarily a bad thing, since if your customer needs to make a few trips to your store to find the absolutely right items for her home, you and your staff have a great chance to make friends with her, and she'll be back.

One drawback is that quite a lot of this merchandise can be very hard to transport and pack.

Be sure you check each piece with your customer before it leaves the store so both parties are aware of any minor defects. When you pack the merchandise, show the customer how to re-pack it so he or she has a better chance of getting it back safely, just in case. This may require using more bubble wrap or packaging than usual but it is worth the extra care.

If you use a delivery service, choose them very carefully to be sure they are efficient, well-priced, tidy, and polite. Make sure the customer knows she is responsible for delivery charges in both directions should she reject the piece. Making the delivery yourself is terrific, since it gives you the opportunity to sell the item in the customer's home.

LET THEM TRY BEFORE THEY BUY

Consider allowing your customer to take larger pieces "on approval." If your customer is not sure the item is what he needs, let your customer bring the merchandise home and see how it looks for a day or two. Customers love this policy because they don't have to have the hassle of a return, and you are showing that you trust them and want to work with them. This policy is handy for you because the customer must decide quickly, rather than taking the full 14 days, and you don't have to ring up a big nasty return if he brings it back. Print an "On Approval" form that includes the customer's name, address, phone, and credit card number. Also have the return date clearly marked on the slip so everyone knows when it must be purchased or returned.

GIFT RECEIPTS

What about those wedding presents? Put a gift receipt in the box that refers to the original transaction but does not show the price. If your computer or cash register cannot do this, keep a simple log and put a numbered sticker on the item that refers to the original sale. Include the purchaser's name and how it was purchased.

DEALING WITH UNREASONABLE CUSTOMERS

Eventually you will have to deal with an irate customer who just can't understand why she cannot return merchandise months after purchase or without price tags or receipts. Try the rational approach. Tell her about your costs of doing business, what your policies are, and that you must be certain it is from your store before you can take it back. This can be unbelievably frustrating, since the customer usually feels she is absolutely in the right.

WHEN TO GIVE IN

Once you start arguing, you've lost your customer, even if you give in at the end. Always accommodate good customers if you possibly can. Tell them they are special and that is why you are making this exception. Sometimes you may give a refund just to avoid a fight ... but remember that there are customers who are impossible to please and that you may not actually want their business.

When you give a refund, you've just given your customer money to spend. Keep her happy so she spends it with you!

33
Making a Buck on eBay

Some days it seems that eBay is everywhere. Everybody knows somebody who got a great deal on a treasure or sold something that seemed worthless for a bundle or replaced a broken heirloom. It is easy to spend hours aimlessly searching eBay; and browsing there is a popular pastime for hundreds of thousands of people every day. Collectors revere it, collectible dealers revile it, and millions revel in the bargains and treasures they find there.

While there are lots of people cleaning out their basements and selling their old things on eBay, basically having a virtual garage sale, there are also thousands of store owners who have improved their sales by using this channel of distribution for new, refurbished, and discontinued goods. In addition to selling merchandise, you will find both retailers and manufacturers using eBay as a marketing tool to build their brands.

In addition to selling on the site, many manufacturers are using eBay as a research tool and an avenue for judging value. Because the majority of merchandise is sold at auction, it can be an easy way to see what people will pay for an item and can help marketers set suggested retail prices.

Some retailers are threatened by eBay and worried that it is another major threat to our industry. There is no question that the easy access to collectibles on the site has changed the value structure for many items, but it has also brought renewed interest to the category. Many collectible stores have found this an excellent way to add to their sales with an international customer base, with some shops reporting that their online sales now far exceed their in-store business in this category. Tabletop stores also report excellent results selling china, both new and replacement, sliver, and crystal.

By no means do I think that eBay will replace gift stores or even that most of our products can be profitably sold through this channel, but it is an opportunity for many of us and a marketing channel worth considering. If you have not visited eBay yet, it's time to take a look. Registering is easy and quick—just go to www.eBay.com and follow the simple instructions which will walk you through the process. Search for items that interest you, things you sell, even things you dream of finding. Shop around for a while to help you become acquainted with the site.

If it has been a while since you surfed on eBay, take another look. eBay is constantly being changed and updated to make it easier to buy and sell, faster to search, and safer to shop. They frequently add new categories and sub-categories, making it simpler to find what you want. I frequently visit eBay just to stay current with the changes and frequently find something I cannot live without.

Make a buck off eBay

Here is an unusual idea from Randy Eller, who heads a consulting firm servicing the Gift and Home Industries.

"The number one opportunity available to Independent Retailers in America today is to enhance their ability to drive traffic into their stores. In today's retail environment, it is difficult to compete with the millions and millions of dollars of advertising being spent to drive consumers into traditional bricks and mortar big box stores as well as to internet retail sites. Independent Retailers have a lot to offer the consumer, from upscale product lines to personalized service. The key to unlocking the retailer's potential is to simply get the consumer in the door."

cont'd on next page

cont'd from previous page

"That old axiom of 'if you can't beat 'em join 'em' is an excellent way to describe the opportunity independent retailers have to connect their businesses to eBay to drive traffic to their stores. One of the fastest growing retail models in America is stores that cater to serving consumers who want to sell product through eBay, but want someone else to do all the work. These 'service centers' take photographs of the items to be sold, list the product, collect the payment, and pack and ship the item to the buyer. All the seller has to do is bring the item into the store for photography and then again to have it packed and shipped and pick up their check. This creates two confirmed visits to the store and the second time the retailer is actually handing the consumer money!

"I strongly recommend all Independent Retailers explore this possibility as a way to drive more traffic to your location."

—Randy H. Eller
President
Eller Enterprises, LLC,

WHAT SELLS ON EBAY?

eBay is a great place to sell hard-to-find things, unusual finds, and discontinued items. Closeouts are also often listed on eBay by manufacturers, retailers, and liquidation companies. Even some reps are selling their samples on eBay. A basic tenet is that if you can describe it, you can sell it. The big questions are how much you can get for it and whether it is worth the time and effort to sell the merchandise on eBay rather than just marking it down in the store. You will probably find that most of the products you carry in the store are not listed on eBay, or they appear there briefly and infrequently, because current inventory does not command a high enough price.

If you are new to the site and see lots of surprisingly low prices on items, relax and check "completed items" to see the final selling prices. (Anyone can surf eBay for current auctions, but you must be a registered eBay user to search for "completed items." This search will show you what items have sold in the last 30 days and for how much. Often the final selling price is determined at the very end of the auction (even in the last seconds!), so the prices during the auction can look deceptively low. Also consider the freight, which often adds a considerable amount to the final price.

If you are shopping on eBay, searching "completed items" is also a good place to learn how much you are likely to need to spend to get what you want. I always check to see what prices items have commanded before I start to bid, so I do not get carried away ... which is easy to do.

SELLING ON EBAY

While some stores sell their regular inventory on eBay, many shops carry products just for their eBay businesses that they do not offer in their stores. eBay is a different market and needs to be considered separately. My guideline, by the way, is that if the items will not sell for more than $15 to $20, as a retailer I won't take the time to list it. You can also bundle several items to achieve a higher retail.

eBay is not just for auctions. There are also fixed price listings, buy-it-now options, and Dutch auctions. Since eBay is by far the largest shopping site in the world, with visitors who stay on the site for hours, an eBay store is a cheap and easy way to get your products in front of millions of customers from all over the world. Christopher Radko has an eBay store, as do many independent retailers. Using an eBay store and PayPal (an Internet service which allows instant payment for eBay purchases), you can have an e-commerce-ready web presence quickly and inexpensively.

A winning combination for many merchants is listing some items at auction (by far the most popular method of selling) and listing others at fixed price in an eBay store. Your eBay store will have your logo and branding and will show the variety of merchandise you carry. Many stores find that customers who shop on their eBay stores then browse the store's proprietary website and often even drive to the real store itself. (The web people like to call it "a brick and mortar," but I still think *real store*.) Consider using an eBay store to help build your brand awareness.

eBay is not the answer to every overstock problem, nor can you sell everything you carry on the site. However, you can lengthen your reach to customers all over the world and increase your sales to existing as well as new customers.

If you are new to eBay and wonder where to start, begin by shopping for things you like and understand. Check eBay for equipment like phones, cameras, and computers. There is even a new site (www.ebaybusiness.com) that specializes in all sorts of used and new business equipment, including point-of-sale systems and fixtures.

Then try selling a few things—old computers and cell phones are very easy to list and sell and will give you a good start. After you give it a try, begin experimenting with the merchandise you sell in your store. Photograph your item for sale with one of your striking displays as a backdrop.

Whether you shop on eBay, sell on eBay, or just take a little tour, it is worth the trip.

Make it work for you.

eBay Seller's On Ramp

Readers of this book may enjoy free consulting services from eBay. The seller's onramp program includes a series of phone calls with eBay selling experts, step-by-step instructions on becoming a successful seller on eBay and personalized guidance and selling tips.

The Seller's On Ramp curriculum

Getting Your Business Started on eBay

Selling Strategies

Listing and Managing your Items

Marketing and Merchandising

Scaling your eBay Business

Personalized eBay Business Review

Call toll free 1–866–304–EBAY between the hours of 7–4 PST (10–7 EST). Source Code: MLC8118.

34
Purchase On Your Own Terms

It is amazing to most people that anyone as frugal as I would suggest you pay for something you can get for free, but purchase orders are an expense well worth incurring. Well-planned purchase orders can help you set retails, place orders with the terms that work best for your store, avoid pricing mistakes, and control your open-to-buy.

It isn't just the department and chain stores with thousands of employees working in hundreds of departments that "drop paper" on their own forms. Even if you are the CEO, principal stock holder, general merchandise manager, senior buyer, visual director, clerical, receiving manager, routing director, stock clerk, bookkeeper, inventory control specialist, and janitor all rolled into one person (or even two), you will still benefit from having an order form that is designed with your business needs in mind.

There are two categories of reasons for designing your own preprinted order forms. The first is to have better control over your retail pricing, receiving, and inventory; and the second is to buy under your terms, not the vendor's.

Learn when to buy!

Some categories have huge margins if you know how and when to buy them. Novelty Christmas ornaments are a great example. When you shop for ornaments, you can often get an early buy discount, dating, free freight and quantity discounts, all on the same order. A seasoned holiday trim buyer told me that she makes her money in that category when she buys the product, not when she sells it.

RETAIL PRICING

Pricing is a top-level job and should never be left to someone who does not understand the process fully. Good margins are your ticket to profitability! To realize the maximum markup on any product, set your retail as you are ordering the merchandise rather than waiting until it arrives. Talk to the salesperson about his suggested retails, consider the freight, and establish your selling price. If your PO clearly states the selling price, anyone can price the goods.

A clear PO also helps avoid mistakes in the stockroom. Years ago, my mother told one of her employees to price some merchandise then add a quarter for the freight. Well, the employee did just that, and the products sold very well at wholesale plus 25 cents. Many things have been mis-marked because they are priced in dozens, and someone who didn't pay attention in the third grade could not divide by twelve to get the cost.

A standard order form gives the employee who unpacks the shipment an easy-to-understand document that clearly details what was ordered, how many there should be, and what the prices are. Include columns on the form to enter quantity received. Have your stock person mark the date received on the form as he checks in the order and list any discrepancies or damages. With a standard form and all the right information, reconciling the PO to the invoice will be very easy for the bookkeeper.

One more thought: as you write the order, if you have any thoughts about displaying the products or merchandising them with other items, make a note on your copy of the PO so you will remember it when the goods arrive.

ELEMENTS OF THE PURCHASE ORDER

A purchase order is a binding contract. When a buyer signs the PO, she agrees to the terms specified on the contract. In turn, shipping the order constitutes acceptance by the manufacturer. Take a look at the various elements on the vendor POs in your files. Each has specific policies that were worked out by their comptroller, credit manager, and/or collections department. Obviously, these were not worked out for the convenience of the retailer. When you make your own order forms you set the rules you need to run your business efficiently.

Review the elements below whether you plan to print your own purchase orders or not. You can always specify your terms on any manufacturer or sales rep's PO.

PURCHASE ORDER NUMBER

Always use a PO number. This is the best way to identify or track your order in any manufacturer's system.

ORDER DATE, SHIP DATE, AND CANCEL DATE

Specify a ship date and a cancel date. Without a cancellation policy, many vendors will ship really old orders, which may arrive long after you have any desire for the merchandise. Also, if there is a shortage of merchandise, many companies will fill the orders with cancel dates first and hold the undated orders to fulfill when more inventory is available.

MANUFACTURER'S NAME AND PHONE NUMBER
REPRESENTATIVE'S NAME AND PHONE NUMBER

You need to know who is invoicing you as well as who is servicing your account and how to reach them in case of errors or reorders. If you are ordering from a rep who uses his own forms, be sure he includes the manufacturer's name and phone number (legibly!) on his PO so you can track the shipment and match the invoice and purchase order.

FOB POINT & SHIPPING INFORMATION

Where is this merchandise coming from? How will it be shipped? As you fill in this blank, ask if you are ordering in the most economical way for freight costs.

Margin boosters

Ask each vendor about programs and special offers that will boost your margins. These might include:

Dating programs

Opportunity buys

Freight programs

White sales

Overstock sales

Closeouts

Seasonal buys

Quantity discounts

Case pack discounts

With some merchandise you may be better off to order more products less frequently and ship common carrier rather than UPS. Ask the salesperson!

This is also the time to inquire about the company's freight policies. With shipping at an all-time high, you need to watch this expense category carefully.

TERMS OF PAYMENT

Net 30? Credit card? Special dating terms? However you plan to pay, put it in writing.

BACKORDERS

Backorders are aggravating to everybody, but almost every company has them at some time or another. You can specify the number of backorders you will accept (i.e., no more than two shipments), the dollar amount (for instance, cancel backorders less than $50), or the freight terms (all backorders must be shipped freight free). Choose the right terms for each situation.

QUANTITY, ITEM NUMBER, DESCRIPTION, UNIT COST, AND EXTENDED COST

These are the basics that tell you what you bought and that give your receiving department the details it needs to receive the order and check for substitutions, mis-shipments, and shortages. You may also want to add category or department numbers if you use them. Next to these columns is the blank column for receivings. Don't forget a total for your open-to-buy figures.

Some large companies have complicated order forms that clearly list what you are ordering. If it is easier on you, use their forms to write the order and attach your own PO to theirs.

DESIGNING AND PRINTING THE FORM

Use your logo and make your form reflect your store's image. Include all your obvious important information, billing and shipping addresses, phone, fax, email, and DUNS number. If you write a lot of special orders that are drop-shipped, have a box for the customer's shipping information.

AND FINALLY …

You'll need three copies of the purchase order: one for the manufacturer, one for the receiving department, and one for the office. Do not show the wholesale cost on the receiving form. I firmly believe that most employees should not know what the gross margins are. Without the knowledge of all the expenses one incurs in running a store, even a keystone markup can look excessive.

These are the basics. You can add routing instructions, additional terms, print your credit references on the back, or modify it any way that works for you.

Your order form will pay off. Honest.

35

Dents, Dings, Damages …
Also Shortages, Shoddy Shipping and
Other Slip-ups

It's not as bad as getting the wrong toy from Santa, but receiving shipments that are not as ordered is expensive, time-consuming, and aggravating.

Even the best and most efficient companies make the occasional error in shipping … and newer manufacturers who are just learning the ropes can be a nightmare. Whether the problem is handled by the vendor efficiently or not, having a system in place at your end will make the whole thing easier.

Check it in on the floor

It is always exciting to open a box and see what is in it, even when you were the one who placed the order. Give your customers the same joy and excitement you felt as a kid at Christmas (or other holiday of your choice) and unpack orders on the selling floor. The commotion draws a crowd and people are always excited to see what's new—even if the product is a reorder. While it may be commonplace for you, it's still fun for shoppers to think they are getting the very first look at a product. What is not fun for them to see is the packing slip or invoice with wholesale pricing, so do your bookwork away from interested eyes.

OPEN SHIPMENTS PROMPTLY

Always unpack orders and check them as soon as you receive them, even if you have ordered seasonal merchandise to be shipped far in advance of the selling season. The faster you act, the easier it is to get the problem rectified. Most companies will not honor any claims made later than ten days after delivery. Additionally, replacement goods may be sold out if you do not act quickly, and if you have paid by credit card you will want to make any necessary claims before you pay the bill with the invoice on it.

COUNT THE MERCHANDISE

Amazingly, many merchants think that their vendors can count better than their receiving clerks. Don't believe it! It is amazingly easy to make mistakes as you pack orders. Always count the merchandise in every shipment, and check it carefully against the purchase order to be sure the merchandise is all there and correct. It is a good idea to check the description as well as the style number to be sure the item in the box is actually the one you wanted. Open the master-packs, look in the boxes, and peer into the bubble wrap.

Check everything carefully against your purchase order.

ENTER ALL INFORMATION ON YOUR PACKING SLIP

When you (or your staff) unpack an order, use the packing slip for notes about the shipment. If the order is perfect, mark it OK; otherwise note the details of the problems clearly. Initial the packing slip so the person reconciling the invoice can ask questions if the notes are not clear. Attach the packing slips and the purchase orders to the invoices so you will know what action to take when you pay the bill.

MAKE A CLAIM FORM!

This is a case where a little up-front work will save you lots of time. Develop a form that you use for all claims. A simple form makes claims easier to place and track and gives the manufacturer all the information they need to take care of the problem. When customer service departments have all the details they need, they can process your claim quickly and easily.

Here's what you need on the form:

+ All store information, including phone, fax, email, and contact name.
+ The date, order number, your account number (found on the invoice or packing slip), and invoice number
+ Type of problem. The basic categories are: short shipment, mis-shipment, defective merchandise, broken or damaged goods. Make a checklist on your form.
+ A place to describe the problem exactly. Leave room for the details.
+ How would you like them to handle the problem? Include a check off list: pick up merchandise, replace merchandise, do not replace merchandise, cancel backorder.

Add this statement to your form: "All merchandise not picked up within 30 days of claim will be donated to charity or thrown away." If the vendor does not issue the pick-up within that time, you can legally dispose of the merchandise. This will help you keep your stockroom clear and prompt the vendor to pick up the merchandise quickly.

Use the form even if you call the company with your complaint. Take notes on it as you talk to customer service and fax it to them as a confirmation.

RETURNS AND FREIGHT

Don't pay to ship the product back! Always ask the company to issue a call tag. You should not have to pay freight both ways for their mistake. Also, if it is a large item and you are not electing to have them replace it, ask for a freight credit as well as the merchandise credit. Replacements should always be shipped freight free.

Proud to be mom and pop

My husband and I are proud to be the owners of a family owned independent store. So proud, in fact, that we sometimes wear shirts in the store with our names on them: Mom and Pop.

DAMAGED IN SHIPMENT

If your merchandise was damaged in transit, you'll have to make your claim to the carrier. Teach everyone on your staff to inspect every box before signing for a delivery and to count the cartons carefully, confirming they were all delivered. If you don't note visible damage or shortages on the receiving documents, making a claim will be much harder if not impossible. When making a claim to a carrier, keep the boxes and packing material for their inspection.

PAYMENT

If you have net 30 terms, it is easy to deduct the correct amount from your invoice. If you have prepaid the order, paid by credit card, or taken a C.O.D. (the worst possible method of payment), you will have to ask for a charge credit or refund from the company. This is usually easy with established companies, but it can get a little dicey with companies that do not have their systems in place. Keep the form in your accounts payable folder (or in a special file) until you have received the credit.

If you do not receive satisfaction from the vendor, contact the credit card company to dispute the portion of the charge that is in question.

REPLACEMENT MERCHANDISE

Many stores write a new PO to cover the replacement merchandise. Note on the PO that the product should be freight free and mention special terms, if any.

What if the company ignores you and your lovely form?

Every time you call or fax, make a note on your form and date it. Always write down the name of the person with whom you spoke at the company and what he said he would do. Keeping careful records will help resolve the dispute in the very unlikely event that legal action is taken.

If customer service does not address the issue, speak to the sales manager, the vice president, or the president. Let your sales representative know what happened, too. Don't start a fight! Keep it polite and to the point.

Little (and big) shipping errors are just part of the magic of owning a store. Handle them efficiently and they will be mere trifles.

36
Phun Phone Phacts

Can you hear me now? You're probably paying too much for your phone service. While this is the one utility where you have lots of choices and can save a great deal of money with careful shopping, the prices are constantly changing. What was a fabulous deal last year may not be so good now. Some experts say you should check prices and plans every three months, but I think once a year is about as often as a normal person can really face the issue.

Get your bills for the last three months. While your current (or even prospective) provider can access this information, I think it helps to have it in front of you on paper as you start to wade through the details. Thanks to the convenience of automatic bill payment, we often forget to check the invoices and see what exactly is on them. Check for unauthorized charges, unfamiliar phone numbers, or anything else you don't understand. Then you can look for potential savings.

Look at the service you have. Are you paying for lots of extras like speed dialing, three-way calling, voice mail, and call forwarding? Do you use these conveniences? If you don't use them, don't pay for them. Review your calling patterns. Are you making lots of calls in-state and paying high toll costs? How many long distance minutes do you use each month? If you make lots of long distance or toll calls, you may want a flat rate service; but if you make very few toll or long distance calls, avoid calling plans with monthly fees or minimums, and opt for a pay-per-minute rate.

When you are familiar with your bill, call your current provider and ask for an account review and suggestions about saving money. Almost every time I do this, I find something that saves me money. Rate plans change all the time, and the companies generally don't tell their customers or change their billing, so it truly pays to ask. Make notes so you can compare the rates with other carriers. Check prices in the following categories: basic service with local calls, toll calls (often a real killer), long distance, international calls, toll-free service, and conveniences like speed dialing. Some carriers also include your high-speed web access in the plan.

Now that you know what you are paying and what you can get from your current provider (or providers), look at your options. You've probably received offers in the mail from other local carriers. You can also compare prices at www.saveonphone.com and www.hometownphone.com. When you find the best deal, ask what incentives the company offers to change service. Give your current company the opportunity to match any offers you get. They will often meet the deal the competition offers to keep you as a customer. If you change companies, the new one will usually pay the change fees and give you an incentive

Yo, Hello?

How does your staff answer the phone? They should all use the same greeting. Write a little script and tell them what to say, then call the store occasionally to hear how they sound. Some phone etiquette experts suggest keeping a mirror near the phone to remind you to smile when you talk. Did you know the other person can hear the smile in your voice?

Cell phone Savvy

If your employees have cell phones, and I am sure they do, ask them to put them away during working time. If your customers use cell phones in the store, pay attention. When they start to annoy other shoppers, suggest they take their conversations outside.

to make the switch change. Remember that they really want your business, and they'll work to get it.

Next move on to your cellular service. Make sure you understand promotions, peak calling periods, area coverage and roaming, and long distance requirements to avoid paying too much. Call them, too. Even if you are still under contract you can often negotiate a better rate on your mobile service. Do you have extra minutes? Use them at the store for long distance instead of the regular line to save money. If you have delivery trucks, multiple locations, or an off-site office, a group or family plan from your cellular provider may be much cheaper than using the regular phone, which will charge you for each local call.

Where does customer loyalty come into all this? Mine went out the window when I discovered that the phone companies don't advise their customers automatically when rates decrease and will happily overcharge their loyal customers.

JUST THE FAX, MA'AM

Remember when a fax seemed like a miracle? When the speed and efficiency was almost unbelievable? I used to run into the office to watch faxes arrive, thrilled with the new technology. Since the advent of email, most of my faxes are offers of vacation packages and mortgage reductions, a total waste of ink and paper. I now receive faxes directly onto my computer so I can delete the junk and print the good ones.

Do you have a dedicated fax line? Do you still need it? You can have several numbers routed through one line and use a distinctive ring so you can tell what kind of call is coming in. I still have the separate fax number that is on my cards and stationery, but having it come in on the voice line saves me a little more than $20 per month.

EQUIPMENT

You will almost always be better off buying your equipment than leasing it. When the time comes to change or upgrade, sell your old equipment on eBay. You can even sell broken items there—technicians will buy them for parts. It is amazingly easy to list and sell old equipment on eBay, freeing cash for the latest innovation. By the way, if your cell phone is broken, lost or stolen, eBay is the place to buy your replacement for far less than the cellular companies charge. If you get a new phone when you sign for another contract, sell the old one on eBay. In addition to making you some money, it is nice to know that the old stuff is going to good use and not a landfill.

ON THE ROAD

After you save all this money at home on the phone, you can easily blow it on one trip. Never, ever, ever use a hotel phone for a direct call unless you check the prices, which are usually usurious. While you can almost always use your cell, the phones don't work in every building; so carry a calling card with a low per-minute rate just in case you need it.

If you travel outside the U.S., add international service to your phone plan before you leave so your family and staff can call you, then cancel the service when you return. A very small monthly fee of several dollars can add up to hundreds in savings. Watch out for credit cards, too. I thought I was saving money by billing a call to my American Express card, but a five minute call from Mexico City cost $42.00. Many cellular companies offer international service for an additional fee. Whatever you do, plan it about a week before your trip so it can take effect. Also be sure you get instructions in your native tongue before you leave the country and try to use your cell phone in a foreign land.

Shopping for better prices on phone service is not an amusing pastime or a rewarding hobby, but it pays off. Take the time to make the calls.

Foreign travel tip

Long distance calling cards are a cheap way to call home from almost anywhere in the world. Buy them at Costco or Sam's Club for the best prices. Another tip—be sure you get the access code you will need in the foreign country and instructions for use before you leave, in English.

V

Making Customers Happy

37
Let Your Customers Go!

Is there something that could make your customers happy and keep them in your store longer? Are you sitting on a big, fat asset that you are refusing to use? There is a simple amenity you can easily provide: let your customers use your bathroom. If you send your customers away when nature calls, they may never return.

Many gift retailers do not permit their customers to use the store restroom. I don't know if they are worried about cleanliness, shoplifting, toilet paper expense, or what; but this is a short-sighted policy. Especially in this retail climate, we need to keep our customers happy and comfortable in the store as long as we can. Don't say no when they have to go!

Restaurants completely understand the importance of bathrooms. Designers of fine restaurants work hard to maintain the ambiance throughout the establishment, with great powder rooms an absolute necessity. They take as much care with the décor and the lighting in the necessary room as they do in the dining room or bar. After all, when one of their customers looks in the mirror, how she sees herself is part of how she will remember the restaurant. If she looks great and the setting is pretty, she is more likely to return.

The men's room at the Madonna Inn, in San Luis Obispo, California, is so famous it has long been a destination for tourists of both genders traveling up or down the California coast. Naturally, when the one million visitors a year stop to visit the gent's, they stay for a snack in the restaurant and may shop in the many stores the property offers. This bathroom is a press agent's dream with visitors from around the world talking about its rocky waterfall and clamshell sinks.

Better department stores almost always have delightful powder rooms where a lady can sit for a few minutes if the rigors of shopping have become too much. I still think longingly of the fabulous marbled ladies' room at I. Magnin in San Francisco. When you stopped there to check your lipstick, you knew you were part of something very glamorous.

While an independent storeowner can hardly be expected to provide a fainting couch or lighted make-up tables, if there is a bathroom in your store you can offer your guests a clean and attractive restroom, as you would in your own home.

If your bathroom is located in your back room or basement, far off the selling floor, you have more work ahead of you to make the facility accessible. If this is the case, arrange your storage area to keep it safe, attractive, and theft proof. Although the layout of some stores makes easy access to the bathroom almost impossible, it is still worth your time to let customers use the bathroom, even if

Where to go for glamour

The ladies' room at The Waldorf Astoria is the most beautiful I have ever seen. Many San Francisco shoppers have fond memories of the fabulous powder room at I. Magnin on Union Square. While far from the most beautiful, the employee's bathroom in a rural grocery store I used shortly before the birth of my son is still one of my most appreciated. 15 years later, I still shop there and always thank the owner for that long-ago pit stop.

you must guide people to the door and monitor them while they pass through the storage area.

Pregnant women and customers with children are the most appreciative of bathrooms, especially during that stage when young children seem to be on a quest to visit every toilet in town. A scrapbook storeowner told me she installed a tiny, child-sized toilet in her store. The kids like it so much they insist that their mothers bring them to the store whenever they are in the neighborhood … and most mothers buy something while they are there.

The owner of a souvenir store told me that she attracts customers to her store with a simple sign that says, "We have clean restrooms." Her store is in a very busy tourist location where most merchants post signs saying that they don't have facilities. She displays area maps and memorabilia in her bathrooms and says the people who visit them almost always make a purchase, even if it's just a few postcards.

Keeping the bathroom clean is important but not critical; you'll be facing nothing worse than the havoc caused by little boys in any home. Remember, you will probably not have a constant stream of people waiting in line for the toilet, so the mess will be minimal. One storeowner told me that most of her customers are so happy they can use the bathroom, they wipe the sink and always leave it looking nice. Still, check the restroom occasionally during the day and be sure you always have plenty of toilet paper, hand soap, and towels. It is also nice to have a counter large enough for diaper changing if you can make it fit. Don't forget to empty the garbage often if you have lots of babies in the store. One more thought: add a covered wastebasket (with a foot pedal) for feminine necessities along with a sign asking your customers not to flush them.

The cost of a few cases of toilet paper and paper towels is a small price to pay for the friendship of your customers in their time of need.

Design your bathroom with the same care you give to the rest of the store. Your necessary room should not look like an afterthought but an important part of your store. The colors and design ethic should mirror the store's, although you can certainly be a little wilder in a bathroom. It is important that the feeling of the store is carried through to the bathroom—keep them in that shopping mood. A beautiful restroom will lift the mood of your staff, too.

Another important point is lighting. Be sure that the mirror is well enough lit for a quick make-up fix. A dark bathroom always looks dingy and dirty, so keep it bright.

The bathroom is a surprisingly good place for display. After all, you have a captive audience with a little time to look around. Arrange posters, framed art, or decorative accessories on the walls. Stationery and scrapbooking stores can exhibit samples of custom invitations or memory book pages. Anyone selling personal care items can provide testers of nice hand soap and lotion. If you are a florist, be sure to have a nice arrangement on the counter. Use your imagination! Obviously, do not display anything small enough to fit into a shopping bag

Note from the proofreader

Proofreading this book makes me want to quit my writing job and go out and open a retail store. I would start by designing a fabulous bathroom. (By the way, you've used the word "fabulous" about 30 times, but I wouldn't be tempted to replace any with synonyms.) The PPR is all about fabulous!

—Sharla Scannell Whalen

or purse. Remember to change the displays in your bathroom, just as you do in other parts of the store.

You might also consider a corkboard to hang the hundreds of notices local organizations want you to publicize ... you can display the posters without cluttering up your window.

If you sell ready-to-wear and use the bathroom as a changing room, don't forget to install hooks and provide a chair or stool.

Your store's bathroom does not have to be on a par with the Ladies' Lounge at Saks. Whatever you can provide will be appreciated. Customer service is the hallmark of a great store, and a clean bathroom is a service we all appreciate.

If you love them, let them go.

38
Six Simple Suggestions

How many times have you heard, "It's the simple things that matter"? Well, it's true. Attention to the small details is what sets a great business apart from the rest of the pack.

Here are a few niceties you shouldn't neglect.

POST YOUR HOURS ON A SIGN
YOUR CUSTOMERS CAN READ FROM THEIR CARS

If your store is in a strip mall or on the street, make sure customers won't need to get out of their cars to read your sign. Many stores use signs with little tiny numbers. Here's what happens: I drive up to the store, and you are not open, so I am irritated. It is a completely unjust aggravation, to be sure, but real. Then I try to read the sign from my car, and I cannot see it without parking, getting out of the car, and walking up to the door. This increases my aggravation level. I'm mad at the store, and I don't want to come back. Unreasonable, but the logical course of action is to fix the sign.

OPEN EARLY

Some stores won't open their doors until the stroke of the hour posted on the window. Why is that? When customers are waiting to get in the store, *let them in!* If you are vacuuming or moving things around, tell them you are happy to have them browse while you do your chores. The only reason to make them wait is if you have cash to be counted or insufficient staff to man the store. If that is the case, open the door and tell them when you will be able to invite them in.

The Costco in our area always opens their doors five to ten minutes early. I was eavesdropping while I was waiting to shop and was amazed at the number of customers who mentioned that the doors usually go up a little early and how much they appreciate it. I also heard one lady who was furious at another big box store for not opening on time, based on her watch and the radio. She was absolutely livid that she had to wait an additional four minutes for them to open. Do yourself a favor: let them (and their money) into the store as soon as you can.

DON'T CLOSE EARLY!

Although we storeowners are always afraid we'll get trapped by an after-hours

Kids at the register

Don't overlook your shorter customers. Many clerks look right over the heads of little kids and completely ignore them. Children with money to spend are real customers—and an investment on the future of your store. Treat them with the courtesy and respect you give grown-up shoppers and they will come back again and again ... and bring their mothers.

browser, reading every card, poking through the store, and keeping us late, don't close the door before the posted hour—especially in the face of somebody who wants to purchase a specific item. These shoppers never forget—either the rejection or the accommodation!

Sometimes people are just killing time in your store, and some shoppers are obnoxious, rude, and basically refuse to notice the clock. You may eventually have to ask them to depart, but remember that the longer they look, the more likely they are to find something. If you absolutely have to leave your store promptly at closing time, be as polite as you can when dislodging lingering lookers.

KEEP YOUR EMPLOYEES OFF THE PHONE

It is exceptionally annoying to be trying to get help from a salesclerk who is on the phone or chatting with a co-worker. Customers are typically reluctant to disrupt someone on the phone or involved in a conversation; but sometimes even when a potential buyer tries to interrupt, she can't get the clerk's attention and may just put her item down and leave the store in a snit. Although this is a tired old issue, it bears repeating.

A newer issue is employee cell phones. Unless you have a part-timer who is also a surgeon waiting for an organ donor to call, tell everyone to leave her phone (turned off) in the car, purse, or coat pocket.

DRESS YOUR STAFF WELL

I love a man in uniform. Actually, I love everyone in uniform … starting with the employees in retail stores. Having a dress code for employees makes them identifiable, helps them look more professional, and adds to the ambiance in your store.

Your store is an environment unto itself. Everything in it, including the staff, should be part of the total look, with the correct colors and theme. Having your staff dressed in their own fashions does not add to the complete picture. At best it is not an addition to the store. At worst it is an embarrassment. I know many shopkeepers who have had to send poorly dressed employees home to change. Some feel that bared midriffs (with or without pierced navels) are acceptable, while others wear torn jeans, sweats, or worse. You can't have your staff looking like they just arrived from a last-chance sale at the thrift shop.

Remember, your customers are in the store to be tempted by the merchandise, not to be distracted by the staff's attire. Talking to your staff about their wardrobes is tricky. You don't want to offend anybody by being critical about his or her taste, but the store comes first.

Enter the staff uniform. This does not have to be a custom suit or high heels and dress. You don't need hats. A simple apron, screened with your store name,

Just say no

Sometimes a customer is tempted to buy something that is just not right for her, for any of a number of reasons (I have a few things in my closet that I certainly should not have been allowed to buy). Say no! Always tell the customer the truth … gently. Tell her if it is the wrong color, too small, not washable or incompatible with small children. She's going to find out and if she doesn't like the item when she gets it home, it will be your fault. If, however, after you tell her she might possibly make a better choice and should reconsider, and she still wants the item, you have done your duty.

is perfect for most stores. Maybe you will decide to upgrade to golf or denim shirts embellished with the store's logo. Do choose something that looks good on everybody so no one is miserable in her new outfit. An added benefit is that in addition to making the staff look good in the store, they will not chance ruining their own clothes.

Some stores find that the logo-carrying garments their staff wears are so popular that they end up selling them in the store. Priced at regular retail, sales of these garments frequently offset the cost of the pieces the staff wears.

Start with matching aprons and nametags. The investment is small, and the professional look is big.

MAKE CHANGE FOR PARKING METERS.

Parking meters increase anxiety. This is an absolute medical fact. Anxious customers browse and spend less, so it is a good idea to help your customers avoid parking tickets.

Make change for those who ask! If a shopper gets a ticket, the bad experience will often drive him away from your neighborhood for months. Meter-feeders will appreciate your help even if they are not shopping in your store. If you don't like to open the register frequently to make change, consider a container under the counter with a few dollars of the correct coins to use solely for making parking change.

"Change with purchase only" or "No change!" signs are unfriendly, which is exactly the wrong image for a store. Some stores even contribute meter money to their customers so they can park free while shopping. Make your store parking-friendly.

NO SMOKING IN FRONT OF THE STORE

If you have staffers who smoke, don't let them indulge in the front of the store. Many stores, restaurants, and even hospitals have a pack of smokers hanging around near the main entrance, sometimes leaving their litter behind. This looks like loitering, obstructs the view of your window, and forces your customers to run a gauntlet to reach the door. Send your nicotine addicts out the back door or down the street. Most non-smokers hate to walk through clouds of second-hand smoke to enter any type of establishment.

O.K., this was a rant about some things that drive me nuts when I shop, but I am one of the legions of customers you serve. Making shopping easier for customers makes a merchant's business better, which makes you more money. Then you can shop and make a list of things that drive you nuts … and send it to me!

39

Don't Touch!!!

Boy oh boy oh boy, do I love a good fight, although not in a store. Recently I asked for creative ways to tell customers not to touch ... and I got some good ones. I also was taken to task by storeowners who encourage their customers to touch.

We'll start with my opinion, since this is my show. Once your customer holds something in her hand, she has connected with it, and the chances of her buying it are increased dramatically. One of the goals of a great display is to make the merchandise appeal to the customer. To make her want to pick it up, pay for it, and take it home. This is a good thing! Use those "don't touch" signs sparingly ... if at all.

People don't like being told what to do, even by a cute little sign or poem. They also don't like to be embarrassed, which is what happens (if they have any manners at all) when they damage merchandise. The ideal solution is to position delicate merchandise so that the customers cannot reach the items without assistance. This way, you don't need a sign (or as many signs) to protect your breakables.

Use glass display cases for delicate or easily stolen merchandise. These fixtures show the product well, help keep it clean, and give you the opportunity to discuss the merchandise with your customer as you show it to her.

Obviously, keep delicate items out of the reach of children and high enough not to be jostled by shopping bags or coats. (Have you seen the Waterford casually displayed on pallets at Costco? How much of that do you think they lose?) One of the sadder realities of our litigious age is that the parent of a child who has destroyed your inventory is likely to sue you for hurting his little darling, so this is doubly important.

My mother, Bert Curtin, had a great method for keeping children's hands occupied in her stores: she gave each child two pieces of wrapped candy, one for each hand. The child had to hold the candy until he or she left the store. She also says if she didn't like the mother, she gave the kids unwrapped candy, but I am almost positive that was wishful thinking.

Many stores encourage touching. Brian Smucker, of Baksheesh in Sonoma, CA, says:

> At the end of your March Giftware News column, you ask for ideas on good ways to tell customers not to touch the merchandise. I sure hope you're kidding. That is the last thing I would want to do. At Baksheesh, we do everything we can think of to make sure customers DO touch the merchandise. We get rid of all packaging except for items with small pieces that might get lost. We put things out on open

Touch the Plush

Stuffed animals have come a long way in the last 40 years. The biggest change is quality and softness of the fabrics. The category has a high profit margin for the retailers as well as the lack of damages—ability to order in the quantities you need, whatever size your store.

Good plush companies should always sell safe, attractive trendy products, which sell to customers of all ages, from babies through tweens. Adults and even seniors will purchase pieces that catch their eye or the fabrics with the softness they can't resist. There is no end to collecting plush, everyone is ready for one more hug!

—Paul V. Roche
Senior Vice President
Aurora World

shelves, rather than behind glass. Jewelry hangs on pegs and is not in a case. We make shelf signs telling people to try things out. We invite customers to play with toys and games and musical instruments.

Texture, feel, touch—these facilitate the sale of a lot of items. It's true for stone, for wood, for table linens, and scarves, for all manner of things. I've seen drums in stores with "do not touch" signs. If I can't play it, how in the world am I going to buy it? Two of our top sellers so far this year, by dollars sold, are finger puppets and beaded glass rings. Both would be slow movers without touching.

Do things sometimes get broken or shopworn? Of course. But the sense of touch, the experience of handling, sells far far more. I think we break more ourselves redoing displays than customers ever do. And by the way, a customer who breaks something does NOT buy it in our store. This is just one of many customer service policies that create a world of goodwill.

Baksheesh is a fair trade retailer of handcrafted gifts from the developing world. Everything we sell (except books and CDs) is handmade. Does our approach work? We will complete our 6th year in June. Every year has been profitable, and every year has shown a double digit increase in sales over the year before.

Here's a similar opinion from Diane O'Connell, Collector's Corner, Rockaway, NJ:

How do I tell my customers not to touch?? I don't!!!! If I don't want it touched, it's behind glass and then I open the doors & let them lift it and see the price. I remember as a collector myself trying to see the price underneath. As for breakage I don't charge them if something happens to break at the hands of their children. Unusual yes, but it works for me and I've been in business for 11 years now.

Sometimes there are things that won't fit in a case, but you really don't want people to touch. Matthew Goodman, George Little Management's display manager, had some terrific suggestions:

I have seen a few creative ways to handle conveying a message to customers not to touch the goods. One is posting a sign in a variety of different languages, the last sentence in English. Ne touchez pas si'l vous plaît, Por favor no toquar, Please do not touch. Years ago a museum had the slogan, "Our artwork was created to touch everyone, but please don't touch the works of art." It seems like that slogan could be translated for a retailing environment, as well. I have also seen a simple sign with a symbol of hand touching a glass vase with the circle and slash as the international "NO" sign through the scene.

One of my co-workers, Mary Stope, went to a craft museum where visitors were encouraged to touch the merchandise only while wearing white gloves supplied by the gallery. The artist wanted viewers to experience the art without spreading oils from the hands on the bronze sculptures. Very interesting.

Other stores supported the hands-off policy. Natae sent a poem:

> *Touch it? Don't try it.*
> *Because, if you Break it,*
> *You BUY it!*

This is, of course, a new version of the much-loved classic:

> *Pretty to look at*
> *Delightful to hold*
> *If you break it*
> *Consider it sold.*

Breakage is one of the inherent costs of doing business in a gift store. While you want to keep the losses as small as possible, too strict a policy will impede sales, so use those signs sparingly. Encourage your customers to touch and try the merchandise. You'll sell more of it ... and that's the whole point.

Don't touch

Do you have a good way to tell your customers not to touch the merchandise? How about a snappy sign that says "Hands Off" in a gentle and caring way? I am looking for great ideas to share. Let me know!

40
Who's Sorry Now?

It's happened to me three times lately, so I'm thinking it is a trend. What has happened to the apology? Why don't staff people in stores and restaurants say they are sorry when something goes wrong?

It should not be a big deal to say "I'm sorry" when there is a minor glitch in service, an error at the register, or a mishap in merchandise delivery. Somehow it seems we are forgetting these words, which follow only "please" and "thank you" as the cornerstones of a civilized society.

⁓

My family and I were waiting for service in a bakery. Several employees ignored us (and several other groups of customers) while they bustled around behind the counter. Nobody said "Hello!" or "Be right with you!" or even "Wouldn't you prefer to eat at the restaurant next door?" which was the implied message.

Finally, my husband spoke up and asked why we had been ignored and treated as if we were unwelcome. Instead of an instantly apologizing, the woman behind the counter was a little snippy as she deigned to serve us. He asked for the manager, and she said she was the manager. He requested her superior's phone number; in lieu of that she directed him to the toll-free number on the receipt.

The next day, still steaming like the coffee we never got, he called the regional office. Finally, after several calls, he spoke to a district manager who apologized profusely, sent us gift certificates, and confided that the person at the counter was actually an assistant manager and this was not the first complaint. We wondered why she was still there, but that is another issue.

So now this company has had to spend time and money to try to mollify a customer when all the situation required originally was a simple, "I'm sorry! I will be right with you!" from the clerk.

⁓

Several days later, again with my family in tow, I checked into a hotel that makes a big deal about their frequent-stayer program, which is supposed to be tailored to each guest's wishes. Our room was not ready, so they very graciously gave us a temporary room so we could change for the pool. The bathroom had not been cleaned. I will spare you the unsavory details, but I mentioned them to the desk clerk, and she said "Oh, I'll call housekeeping." Had she said something like, "EEWWW! Gross! I am so sorry," I would have felt much better and instantly forgiven them. Let me just state, it was *really* gross.

Our second room was clean, but it was not the room we had been promised. The treats that were supposed to welcome us on arrival were not delivered to the room until 10:30 the night before we departed, waking the children. As I checked out, I told the desk clerk the problems we had had. Did anybody apologize? No. Do we plan to return to that hotel? Maybe not. Every one of the three issues was minor, but the lack of interest on the part of the staff was major.

∽

The final missing apology came (actually, it didn't come) from a department store. At a trade show, I unpacked a new sweater and discovered the security tag still firmly in place. Since I always travel very light, this had a big impact on my wardrobe plans for the trip. When I went back to the department store, the clerk removed the tag when I showed her the receipt, but once again offered no sympathy or apology.

In the first situation above, the clerk was most likely just an unpleasant person, and since she is probably hopeless we will sensibly ignore her. The other two cases clearly involved poor training. When a customer makes a complaint, it doesn't matter if the clerk receiving the complaint was at fault. As the representative of the company, he or she must apologize. Often, a sincere apology and acknowledgement of the inconvenience suffered will conciliate the customer. In fact, clerks doesn't actually have to care, they just have to *pretend* to care convincingly. They should have "Act as though you care" tattooed on the inside of their eyelids. How hard should it be to pretend you commiserate with a customer?

Mistakes happen all the time, every place, and really should not be a big deal for a clerk to acknowledge. In each of my examples the problems were minor and would have been forgotten immediately if they were handled well. If they had been handled really well, they would have converted me from a crabby consumer to a devoted customer.

When there is a problem, the first thing the customer wants is acknowledgement. He or she wants to hear that yes, there was some difficulty, and that it is real. This is why, psychologically, a customer will respond better when the word "really" is included in the clerk's response.

Next comes the apology, immediately followed by the resolution. That is really all there is to it, although I suggest throwing in a little sympathy (or a gift certificate, if appropriate) for good measure. Once the customer knows the salesperson is on her side and trying to fix the problem, it is hard to stay mad.

Many studies have shown that a customer who has had a problem successfully resolved becomes a more devoted customer than one who has never had a difficulty. If your staff is aware of this, perhaps it will become easier to say that initial, "I am so sorry!" that should be the beginning of the process.

So here is what I think all of us should teach our staffs:

Pahlow's Policy

This little gem is from Mark Pahlow of Archie McPhee in Seattle.

"With new hires I emulate General Patton and tell them the way it is loud and clear, so there are no misunderstandings.

"I tell them I am not their mother, their father, their therapist, their drill sergeant or their buddy.

"Working here is voluntary and they come here of their own free will.

"There are conditions: if they goof off, steal, lie, come in late, drunk or stoned, do stupid or unethical things, they are out. No warnings, no probation, no discussion. They need to manage their own time, their own lives and their own morale.

"We are here for one thing, to satisfy needs at a profit, not to take care of them.

"And the company has expectations—they be competent, honor agreements, be supportive—not critical, be rational—not arbitrary, and be involved and engaged, so that they have fun, time flies and they get the job done.

"Every once in while one goes pale or faints and quits on the spot, which is great for all concerned.

"Most are thrilled to have such clarity and become extraordinary employees and people."

*Mark L. Pahlow
President
Accoutrements/Archie
McPhee & Company*

I have apologized for thousands of mistakes, many of them my own. It gets easier with practice.

1. Don't take a customer's complaint personally. The complaint is actually lodged against the business, not the person on the phone or behind the counter. Of course, that is hard to do when the lady is screaming at you, but the quick apology will help diffuse the anger. And remember, if you don't care, fake it!

2. While at work, an employee represents the entire company. As that representative, a staff member must stay calm, controlled and not get angry back at the customer no matter how unreasonable he or she may be.

3. This is a chance to be a hero for the customer. Go for the glory.

4. That's not my fault," "I didn't do it," or "My Bad" are not acceptable substitutes for "I am sorry."

Now that we have discussed the simple apology, let's also remember to emphasize the use of "please" and "thank you." I am afraid that those words are the next to be endangered.

I am so sorry I had to write this. Thank you for reading it to the very end. Please read it to your staff.

VI

Memorable Merchants

41
Lessons From My Mother the Retailer

There is no swifter or more direct route into the gift business than birth. Many famous merchants grew up above the stores their parents owned. I didn't grow up over the store, exactly, but I am definitely in this business because of my heritage.

My mother, Bert Curtin, has always been a little unusual. During World War II, she enlisted in the Marines and became an air traffic controller at the Marine Air Base, Parris Island, South Carolina. After the war, she went to school in New York, the first member of her family to attend college. She married my father in 1947, and they moved to Chicago, where she became a successful interior designer.

When I was born, she continued to work and often took me with her. I spent many happy hours on decorating jobs, in her studio, and (best of all) at the Merchandise Mart in Chicago. This was at a time when few women worked outside the home, and I credit my mother with teaching all three of her children, and several of my friends, that women can, and often should, have careers.

My father's company moved us west to Santa Barbara, and when I was in high school she opened the first of her two stores. I was lucky enough, at 14, to begin an apprenticeship at her side as a buyer, manager, salesperson, stock clerk, and display person. I also emptied garbage, swept the floors, and unpacked thousands of boxes.

Finishing Touches was a great success. Our goal was to have the perfect finishing touch for every room in your house. We later added personal care, ready-to-wear, and jewelry. A second store, At Home, came along later and housed the bath shop.

I often quote my mother and share her retail theories in seminars and columns. Here I offer you a little guidance from my mother.

NEVER SAY I

It amazes me that so many employees say, "I have that" when referring to the merchandise in a store. Who owns the inventory? The bank, the store owner, the manufacturer who has not yet been paid … lots of people have a stake in the ownership. Everyone in a store should always say WE whether you are taking credit or blame. Salespeople saying "I" drive my mother crazy to this day.

Another point—never address your mother by her first name at work (or anywhere really). Trying to get her attention one busy day, I finally shouted, "Bert!" and she roared: "I am not Bert! I am your mother!"

TRUST YOUR GOOD REPS

My mother found her location in late summer, so we had to move quickly to open in time for the holidays. She launched the store as a Christmas shop and did most of our buying from two companies. One company sold us far too much product for our fledgling business (I think we still have some of it, 35 years later), and we never bought from them again. The other rep, Roger Gruen, sold us exactly what we needed from Kurt Adler. We sold through most of the merchandise at full retail, had just enough for the sale, and ended up with carry-over that fit in a grocery bag. Roger E. Gruen, Inc. was always our first stop for holiday product. A good rep is an invaluable tool for growing your business. Visit Roger in space 943 at the L.A. Mart, email sales@rogergruen.com, or call 800 734-XMAS.

KNOW YOUR PRODUCT

My mother always learned as much as she could about the products in her store and educated her staff as well. Selling is easy when you know what you are talking about. Read the catalogues and ask your reps about the products they sell.

ALWAYS LOOK GOOD WHEN YOU GO OUT

Do you realize that you run into your customers all the time? Always look good when you are out and about—your appearance is a reflection on your store. Although my mother sold her stores almost 20 years ago, she still sees customers who remember her, the store, and the fun they had shopping there.

IF YOU WEAR IT, YOU'LL SELL IT

At a time in Santa Barbara when ladies were still wearing gloves, hats, and pumps, my mother began offering ready-to-wear in her store. We carried dresses from India with embroidery and mirrors, hand-woven suits from Finland, and appliquéd skirts with entire villages embellished on them. The women who bought them were thrilled that they didn't have to wear stockings or gloves (let alone girdles), but they never would have tried the clothes on if my mother (and her staff) weren't wearing them (and looking fabulous).

If you sell jewelry, scarves, reading glasses, clothing, or even aprons, wear them in your store! I recall several buying trips that were paid for by the clothes my mother wore to the show—and sold to other buyers.

YOUR STORE IS A DESTINATION

Trade magazines often write about "retail-tainment," usually referring to big budget stores with lots of expensive display props and costumed help. Well, that is only part of the equation. Many independent retail stores provide entertainment, escape, and even therapy to their customers. You are selling more than the product you display—you are selling your personality and the fun of visiting your store. Make your shop an extension of you.

BRING YOUR KIDS AND DOGS TO WORK

Is there a baby in a playpen? A dog under the counter? A child at the wrap desk doing his homework? Your store is part of your life (a really big part) and your family should be part of your life at the store. It's good for the kids, the dog loves to be with you, and the customers enjoy seeing well-behaved kids and animals. However, if the dog or the child growls at the customers, make other plans.

MAKE A STATEMENT WHEN YOU BUY

You need to have enough product to sell in order to stay in business. When my mother wanted to add a new department to the store, she researched the manufacturers, chose those that were the best, and bought a wide assortment of the line. Whether it was sequined skirts or toilet seats, we had a good selection, knew the product well, and the category looked important.

WATCH WHAT YOU BUY AFTER FOUR O'CLOCK

As we were unpacking some rather questionable products, my mother realized that we had ordered the merchandise during a late-night, shop-until-you-drop evening in a mart building in Los Angeles. She said, "You know, we shouldn't buy when we are tired. A lot of the product we order late in the day at the shows is not great, and just about everything we bought in the showrooms after 6:00 p.m. is a flat out mistake."

BUY YOUR SEASONAL PRODUCT EARLY

Dating programs are a terrific way to increase your margins, assure delivery of limited production items, and help you plan for the season early. In the years we were selling Christmas merchandise, my mother was religious about placing her orders early in the season. She said, "It's not just the terms and the delivery. If I wait too long to buy, I start to think the ornaments are cute again and always over buy. It is much better to place my orders early while I'm still sick of Christmas."

Not every child raised in a store will end up in the business. My brother and sister are both successfully employed outside the gift industry. My father did end up working in the store after he retired and still holds the record for largest single ready-to-wear sale, which completely contradicts the know-your-product theory. In his case, I think big blue eyes and a simple, "That looks very nice on you" were all that were needed to close the sale.

Independent retail is a cornerstone of our economy and our heritage as Americans. I am thankful that I was reared by a retailer who taught me the value of hard work, gave me the courage to take risks, and inspired me to own my own business.

42

My Husband the Retailer

Penny Pinching Retailers know that running a tight ship is a major key to financial success. My husband, who owned retail stores for 28 years, is an excellent buyer and merchant. He is also prudent, frugal, and downright cheap, qualities that kept his business alive during the lean years and more profitable in the good ones. This column was inspired by his penny-wise ways. While he has declined to be named, he has reluctantly allowed me to write about him. We'll just call him "Steve."

Steve's store was located in a charming suburban downtown area that was once a retail magnet, with dozens of delightful boutiques and two major anchor stores. In about 2,000 square feet, he sold an assortment of product that ranged over the years from stickers to fudge to furniture. He closed the store at the end of 2001, just nine months before the one remaining anchor in town finally shuttered. The area is now a haven for service businesses, restaurants, and offices.

START OUT CHEAP

Don't wait until you need the money to start cutting costs! Look at your business carefully to curb wasteful spending. Your bottom line will benefit immediately, and you'll be better prepared when the business hits a slow period. Comparing prices on supplies, ordering carefully to get the best prices on merchandise and rates on freight are procedures that should be basic in any business.

DON'T GO CRAZY WHEN BUSINESS IS DOWN.

Every business has slow periods (some just don't know it yet), but in most cases they are temporary. It is so easy to be alarmist and go nuts when you have a few bad daily totals. Do all you can to improve your sales, but try not to let it make you insane. Most of us have families as well as stores ... let the kids drive you crazy instead.

DON'T STOP BUYING WHEN BUSINESS IS DOWN

When business is slow, a natural tendency is to tighten up and stop buying, in the hope that your customers will buy what is currently in the store. Your customers are probably as tired of the old merchandise as you are. When business

I am the world's worst salesman, therefore, I must make it easy for people to buy.

—F.W. Woolworth
(1852–1919)

is down, you must keep new merchandise coming in. Have a big sale to free some cash, cut corners elsewhere; but keep your store looking current and exciting.

STAY CURRENT WITH YOUR CUSTOMERS

A retail store evolves over time. The concept you had when you started may not be what your customers want today. In his 28 years in business, Steve's store transformed itself several times. He started as a tropical plant store in 1973, moved into gifts in 1974, added kitchen goods (until the big box stores cut the margins and killed that business), became a trend store in the eighties selling wind-up toys, stickers, cards, and candy, and had become a home accents store in the final years. His path through the gift industry reflected the patterns of the market as a whole and kept pace with the changing demographics of his trading area. Look at your customers and the community you live in to be sure your store serves them well. Be open to change.

DON'T FORGET YOUR CORE PRODUCTS

Greeting cards were a mainstay of Steve's business from the beginning. The early eighties were the glory years for greeting cards, but the category was always a draw for his store. Don't drop a product just because sales are not what they once were. If it still justifies the floor space and your customers look to your store for the category, continue to carry it.

WASH YOUR OWN WINDOWS

The most recent estimate for window washing at Steve's store was $120 per month, for four outside washings and one interior. That is $1440 per year! Naturally, he always did his own windows. After an initial outlay of $60.00 for professional window cleaning equipment, his approximate savings over 28 years was over $20,000. Look at what you pay for any service, from window washing to basic accounting work, and see if the money is truly worth the convenience.

Living by the Rules

My husband says I have lots of rules. He's right. I have terrific rules and the world would be a far better place if everyone listened to me. Well, perhaps I overstate, but heck, it's my book.

PAY YOUR BILLS ON TIME

Good credit is absolutely essential to a well run business. If you want your store to get good service from your vendors, you must pay your bills on time. Make reasonable sales projections and maintain your open-to-buy accordingly so that you are not drowning in receivables. Many store owners pay their bills with credit cards. This can be great, especially with free air miles; however, you must pay the cards in full every month. The astronomical interest rates are an expense no store can afford to incur.

NEGOTIATE EVERY NEW LEASE

As the customer count diminished in Steve's trading area, business naturally went down. When the time came each year to renew his lease, Steve always approached the landlord with a list of what he wanted … and several years he actually received a reduction in rent due to economic conditions. The fact that he was well prepared and always paid the rent punctually helped him in his discussions with the leasing agent. Remember that you negotiate a lease, you don't just accept the landlord's terms without at least trying to get some of your own.

PROTECT YOURSELF FROM EMPLOYEE THEFT

Retailers lose more merchandise to employee theft than shoplifting … and that does not even begin to take into account monetary fraud. Put security measures in place for your cashiers, let everyone know that you are aware of missing inventory, and have frank discussions with your staff about theft. It is easier to prevent than prosecute.

So what is The Husband doing now, you may ask? Well, he has remodeled our house, single handedly. And talking about opening a new store.

43

I Can See Clearly Now

This is a slightly different kind of retail story. Actually, it isn't really retail at all, but since it includes all the components of a successful transaction, I am sharing it. It involves a large, really important purchase and a choice between a high profile establishment and a lesser known enterprise—between a big box and an independent. This time the customer (yours truly) was the winner all around.

I recently had Lasik eye surgery and freed myself from the tyranny of eyeware.

As a penny pincher, I just hate to overspend on anything. Here in southeast Michigan, we look to our Canadian neighbors in Windsor for good prices on lots of things. It is a short commute from Detroit, and the U.S. dollar is strong. Factoring in Canada's longer experience with laser eye care (Canadian ophthalmologists have been performing Lasik surgery for over 20 years), I was sure that I could find excellent care for less money across the border. On the other hand, there are a few areas where one should never cheap out, like medical care, fine jewelry, and real estate—so price was certainly not my only concern.

First I went to a well known, highly acclaimed clinic. I was ready to commit. I would have had the surgery that very day, if I could. But I wasn't quite happy there. While nothing was exactly wrong, nothing was particularly right. The staff was pleasant, but not especially attentive to the patients, and there was a lot of waiting around. The young doctor who examined my eyes annoyed me instantly, calling me by my first name while referring to himself as Doctor So-n-So. After the examination, the next step in the process was a visit with the closer, to schedule the surgery and (primarily) get the payment. Frankly, I was almost ready to be asked whether I wanted electric windows or a buyer protection plan. To my surprise, the price was higher than I expected.

The situation wasn't right; I wasn't comfortable, so I left. Soon after, someone from the clinic called and offered me a discount if I booked the surgery within the next two weeks, but I wasn't going back to that office regardless of price.

IT PAYS TO SHOP AROUND

Then I saw the ad for Dr. Richard Bains. Dedicated to making his service affordable, his Lasik Vision Correction Center bases the price on the correction,

Hot item

Do you sell reading glasses? As the baby boomers age, these fashion accessories are becoming essential. Due to their undocumented migratory habits, causing them all to accumulate in a drawer that is not anywhere near the reader himself, the average consumer over the age of 50 needs seventy-five pair.

charging varying prices which correspond to the difficulty of the operation. My surgery, which wasn't the cheapest, was one-third the price of the first quote.

But that isn't why I chose them.

CUSTOMER SERVICE

At the Lasik Institute, a real live person answers the phone when you call! A nice person, who sends you information promptly and schedules your appointment. Everyone at this office was lovely. From the first phone call to the follow-up visit the day after, every employee I met was pleasant, helpful, and kind. They remembered my name and seemed happy to get my business and determined to make the experience as agreeable as it could be.

The literature they sent answered most of my questions and explained the procedure perfectly. At each step along the way, the staff made certain that I was comfortable and fully informed. The process was quick and efficient—very little waiting in the office.

PRESENTATION

The office was stunning, with handsome furnishings and a knock-out view of the Detroit skyline. The staff was neatly dressed in matching scrubs with the clinic's name on them. It was clear from the moment we entered that this was a first-class office.

QUALITY

Dr. Bains has excellent qualifications and lots of experience. He examined my eyes, answered my questions, and pronounced me a good candidate. Just before the surgery, he asked again if I had questions or concerns. I never felt rushed. I'd go back to Dr. Bains and his office in a second if I had another set of eyes. Since I don't have another pair of orbs to fix, I am sending all my visually challenged friends to him.

When I complimented Dr. Bains, he thanked me and asked what they could do better. He said they are always trying to improve and appreciate comments from their patients.

CUSTOMER SATISFACTION

As we were driving home, my husband and I were discussing what an impressive

Take a look at your business through your customer's eyes

Is your staff friendly?

Are they professional looking?

Are your procedures efficient?

Does the store look, smell and sound good?

Are your prices fair? (good margins and unfair prices are not mutually exclusive)

Do your customers feel important?

And most important of all, do your customers want to come back? That is the biggest test of success.

experience it had been to patronize a business that did everything right, from the first contact on the phone to careful post-surgery instructions.

In the gift business, we are more fortunate than Dr. Bains. His patients don't need to come back, but our customers can return again and again.

Any business, whether selling gifts or improving the gift of sight, has common goals: attention to detail, dedication to giving the consumer a high quality product at a fair price, and the determination to make the experience pleasant. Sending a happy customer (or patient) out into the world is the best advertising there is.

44
The Gift of Giving

One of my heroes died just before Thanksgiving 2002. Bert Tonkin was a star in our industry, a wonderful friend, a loving father and grandfather. He built a terrific company, Western Exhibitors, reared two lovely daughters, and made untold scores of friends.

Bert amazed me (and everybody who knew him) with his attitude about his illness. He was unceasingly upbeat. Bert always said he felt great, which was certainly not always true, and never let the fight for health stop him from working and laughing. It was always fun to be around Bert Tonkin.

While his charitable contributions were immense, it was the giving of himself that prompted the board of Gift for Life (the gift industry's arm of the American Foundation for AIDS Research) to name a special award for him. The Bert Tonkin Gift of Giving Award honors people who have offered more than their money: they have given their time, their work, and their hearts.

Bert Tonkin was an example of a truly kind and charitable individual, in matters large and small.

All of us in the gift industry are privileged to work in a business that is all about giving. While many of us feel that we are unable to make a significant dollar contribution to a cause, there is something every one of us can do for someone else. As you are planning your promotions and marketing schedule, add at least one event that benefits a special cause. While you are shopping a show, keep an eye open for cause-related merchandise that works well with your product mix.

GIVING IS GOOD FOR BUSINESS

Studies by Cone/Roper showed that approximately 80% of Americans would switch to a product, store, or company that was involved with a good cause, if other factors were equal.

This is a trend that helps people feel good about shopping, increases sales for stores, and raises needed money. Everybody wins!

In addition, employees like to be part of charitable efforts. Research conducted by the Points of Light Foundation indicated that company volunteer programs promoted company loyalty and improved employee moral. Involve your staff as you choose the organization you will benefit and develop the programs.

CAUSE-RELATED MERCHANDISE

Enesco, Roman, Syratech, and NCE are just some of the big name companies

Gift for Life

Gift for Life (GFL) was founded in 1992 by a small group of gift and home accessories industry professionals who felt compelled to respond to the tragic loss of friends and colleagues to AIDS. Since then, this group has grown in numbers and gained significant visibility within the gift industry, while raising nearly $4 million for life-saving AIDS research and education.

Gift for Life activities include special events, cause-related marketing, promotions, and the solicitation of corporate and individual donations.

Managed by a volunteer Board of Directors, who donate their time, energy, and resources to the fight against AIDS; current members include manufacturers, retailers, trade mart and trade show executives, publishers, and public relations professionals. GFL is active at market centers nationwide. All proceeds from Gift for Life activities support amfAR, the Foundation for AIDS Research. Gift for Life accomplishes its mission in cooperation with the American Foundation for AIDS Research (amfAR).

which are producing cause-related product. This includes a wide variety of merchandise in which a percentage of the retail price is donated to a cause or charity chosen by the manufacturer. Often these programs include publicity campaigns, celebrity endorsements, and special packaging. This merchandise affords a full retail mark-up, excellent brand appeal, and an emotional connection to the customer.

When you sell cause-related product, it is very important to draw attention to the specifics. Use clear signage to identify the cause, explain it to your employees, ask the vendor for promotional pieces, and inquire about events other stores have given to promote the product. Find the local chapter of the organization that the product benefits and send them the information about the merchandise and your store for their newsletter. Talk to the local volunteers about a special event to publicize their group, draw attention to the charity, and sell more of the product.

About amfAR

American Foundation for AIDS Research (amfAR) is the nation's leading nonprofit organization dedicated to the support of AIDS research, AIDS prevention, treatment education, and the advocacy of sound AIDS-related public policy. Since 1985, amfAR has invested nearly $220 million in support for its programs and awarded grants to more than 2,000 research teams worldwide.

SPECIAL EVENTS

Work with the Junior League or another non-profit group to hold a benefit at your store. These events take careful planning, but charity sales events are very profitable for the store as well as for the causes they support. Ask a spokesperson from the charity to attend (or even speak) at the event to tell your customers how the money you are raising will be used. Consider having a launch party for a new collection of limited edition pieces or a holiday shopping kick-off. In addition to the sales on the night of the event, your store will generate long-term good will in the community and recognition by the non-profit to its donors. Many manufacturers (especially in the collectibles field) can give you excellent advice on staging a special event featuring their merchandise.

Choose your charity carefully for maximum impact—be sure that there is a wide enough base of customers to support the cause. Look for a cause with national recognition or great local importance.

YOU DON'T HAVE FAR TO LOOK

There are plenty of terrific causes in your hometown that need help, and it's not all about raising money. Many worthwhile causes need recognition and publicity. Publicize the arts: do a great window to celebrate community theater, a new installation at the museum, or opening day at the zoo. Many theater companies will lend you costumes, scenery, or props for your displays. A window dedicated to the Girl Scouts at cookie time or the high school football team during their fundraiser will sell related merchandise and support the cause with no cash outlay on your part. Plan these promotions well in advance of the date so you can shop the shows for merchandise to support the theme.

GIFT FOR LIFE

AIDS has a continuing and rapidly worsening impact on the world we live in and on our industry. Gift for Life, the gift industry's own charity, was founded in 1992 by Peter Schauben and Chuck Yancy. It has raised almost four million dollars for AIDS research and education, with 100% of the proceeds going directly to amfAR, the American Foundation for AIDS Research.

There are many convenient and easy ways to support Gift for Life (GFL). Look for cause-related merchandise that benefits GFL, attend one of their fabulous events at a trade show, or call them to help you plan a special promotion in your store. In 2001, board member Cathy Steele and her husband Alan (both of George Little Management) ran the New York Marathon and raised over $40,000 in sponsorship money.

GFL is the only charity solely dedicated to our industry. At the risk of sounding like a commercial, Gift for Life is a tremendous organization. We need you! Visit www.giftforlife.org for the full story.

AIDS WALK EVENTS

Here's a perfect fundraising idea for a gift store, with half the promotion already built in. When your city has an AIDS Walk, donate a percentage of that day's sales on all or specific merchandise to Gift for Life. These walks draw tremendous crowds of people who are looking for ways to help fight this disease; their mood is upbeat, and they will be ready to spend. As well as raising money, an AIDS Walk fundraising event will introduce your store to new customers.

Bert Tonkin helped fund major charities, and he counseled individuals facing the cancer they shared. You can make a difference, whether it is to one person or a thousand.

Be like Bert.

Lucille

My friend Marge Ellis also told me about Lucille, a homeless lady she befriended. The woman had been waiting near the Greyhound station for the last 40 years for her boyfriend, who said he'd be right back. Marge would let Lucille keep some of her possessions under a skirted table in the store, held the lady's money so she wouldn't lose it or get robbed, and let her use the store phone to call the FBI every time President Reagan came to town.

I said that was a lovely friendship, but how did it help her business? Marge said, "Oh, I don't know. It sure made me feel good, though." Do something kind—it will make you feel good, too.

45
Memorable Merchants

What makes a merchant terrific? Why do some stores make you want to return again and again, and others give you the urge to bolt as soon as you receive your change? It is an attitude, a feeling that comes from the owners, and resonates throughout the business. As I listed the companies to profile in this chapter, I analyzed what these dissimilar businesses have in common. I realized that the shared quality is a graciousness towards their customers. Whether it is a little gesture like a cup of water or a big event like a dinner dance, all of these companies show their customers how much they appreciate their business. They treat their customers like guests.

C. LEIGH'S FAVORITE THINGS
Hubbard Lake, Michigan

While antiquing "Up North," as Michiganders say, my neighbor took me to a fabulous store. C. Leigh's Favorite Things is in a delightful old postmaster's house, nicely landscaped, with interesting accessories in the yard and around the building. You enter through a porch and walk into a lovely home, with lace curtains and gleaming wood floors. It truly looks like someone still lives there—someone who has a lot of stuff. Really a lot of stuff. The kitchen has a counter and sink, there's a big table in the dining room, and there are beds in the rooms upstairs. While many stores try to look like real homes, this one actually accomplishes it. Each room is filled with interesting products, mostly old, some reproductions.

The day we visited, Cheri Schiellerd, the owner, was sitting in a window seat working on her books. She chatted with us as we shopped, and we felt as though we had dropped in on a friend. Her assortment is eclectic, and the merchandise was very well tagged (in addition to the prices and descriptions, some items even bore the names of the estates from which she had purchased them). Cheri is very knowledgeable about the antiques she sells and is quite helpful with the details. She has an extensive collection of vintage chenille bedspreads, each neatly bagged and marked with the size, price, and pertinent details. Also in each bag is a copy of a magazine article with a photo and description of the pattern. Cheri's prices were lower than the magazine's suggested prices, by the way.

Cheri has a wide spread of price points, too. When I returned to the store with my then 12-year-old son and my neighbor's 7 year old, each found things in his price range. Evan loved his $1.50 rainbow trout pen.

Each November, after the summer people leave, Cheri has a big sale, marking everything in the store 20% off. She says this helps her clear out old merchan-

Judy Patterson

My very first real job was at a gift store called The Stone Balloon, working after school and on Saturdays for Judy Patterson. Judy is a great merchant and has won many industry awards for both that store in Santa Barbara and her next store, Paddington Station in Ashland, Oregon. Judy's stores were creative and fun, with terrific personality.

Judy taught many important lessons: Use every inch of paper on a roll of gift wrap, never lurk behind the cash wrap waiting to ring up sales when you can get out and talk to the customers and that retailing is a wonderful career. Judy has now sold both stores and has since had many adventures. She also proves that it never gets out of your blood—she eagerly offered to fly to Michigan to work at our new store during set up, unpacking, marking product and hauling garbage. She is one of my retail heroes.

dise, gives her local customers a bonus, and provides a much-needed boost in sales in a quiet month.

After my two visits to her store (there was too much to see on one trip), I felt like we were old friends. This is a house I'll visit again! (C. Leigh's Favorite Things is open seasonally, May to November.)

NORDSTROM
Seattle

This August, Nordstrom's Seattle windows celebrated one of the core philosophies of their business: customer service. The windows featured beautifully dressed mannequins performing services for the customer. There was a washing machine spilling diamonds, reminding customers that ring cleaning is free in the jewelry department; there were children with free shoe department balloons; a mountain of wrapped gifts; and a very handsome shoe shine man. Did you know that the Nordstrom valet will clean your car windows and vacuum your car while you shop?

My very favorite window was a telephone operator besieged with telephone handsets and cords, answering numerous calls and looking frazzled. The message was "During store hours, Nordstrom operators will be there to answer your call." A living, breathing telephone attendant answering the phone is the sign of a store that cares.

While most shoppers realize and appreciate the superior service at Nordstrom, it was impressive to see it so well publicized. Be sure your customers know what you do for them!

AIRLINES PARKING
Detroit Metro Airport

Airport parking is a competitive business, and recent years have been difficult in all travel-related industries. While cutting prices will certainly help attract customers, lowering margins is disastrous for the bottom line; and a dollar or two doesn't mean much to the repeat business traveler, especially if he or she is on an expense account. There are lots of off-site parking lots around any airport, all with similar prices.

Airlines Parking gives great service. When you arrive in the very early morning, they have free newspapers. Frequent parkers do not receive a margin-harming discount, but they get to park at the very front of the lot, eliminating long rides in the buses. Their vans run frequently and their drivers not only handle the baggage, they wait at night until your car starts. My favorite treat is in October, when they have a pumpkin for each departing customer. Their latest amenity is a bottle of ice cold water for each customer to drink on the plane. Unlike the airlines in the skies, Airlines Parking is increasing their amenities. By the way, they will jumpstart your car in the absolute dead of winter, for no charge, should that be necessary.

Preferred parking spaces, efficient service, and cold bottled water? They have built a big repeat business.

Specialty Shop Retailing

For a great reference book about all things retail, buy Specialty Shop Retailing, by Carol Schroeder. An experienced merchant, Carol has put her years of experience into one book that answers many of the questions both novice and experienced shopkeepers ask. She answers more than a few they may not know to ask, too.

Specialty Shop Retailing
John Wiley & Sons

THE DENVER MERCHANDISE MART

This was my first trip to the Denver show in years, and it was a remarkable experience. When I saw the mounted police in the parking lot, I knew I was someplace different. The building staff is delightful and easy to locate if you need directions. There are some terrific showrooms and one of the largest selections of Native American, rustic and lodge style, and western products in the country, as well as most of the leading lines in the gift industry.

This is a mart dedicated to its buyers: they serve a free buffet dinner with live music three nights during the show, with dancing on two nights. These are fun parties! The food is good, and the buyers and exhibitors have a great time. The Denver Mart also provides a lounge for the buyers, with snacks, storage bins, and an Internet connection. Visit www.denvermart.com for more information and show dates. As their speaker, I felt like a movie star when I discovered a gift basket from the meeting planner in my room.

WYNDHAM HOTELS

Wyndham has a free frequent guest club called Wyndham by Request—and you don't even have to stay there frequently. When you register for the club, you tell them your room type and location preferences, what kind of pillow you prefer, and what your favorite snacks are. They automatically assign you the correct room type, with the amenities you prefer, including a welcome snack and beverage. Additionally, members receive huge benefits: free long distance calls, copies, and high-speed Internet service.

When you proceed to a room that is in the location of your choice, then walk in to find the right pillows and a delicious snack, you know that your host has tried to make you comfortable and happy. Wyndham's club makes a guest feel pampered.

❧

Every one of these businesses has found a way to make their customers feel special and important. They have considered carefully what their guests want and how to make the time spent in their establishments more pleasant.

46
Tips from the Big Guys

We've all heard the old saw about the three most important things in retail: location, location, location. Well, it may be almost impossible to surmount a rotten location, but plenty of businesses with terrific real estate have failed. Others have beaten the odds and flourished in odd spots. Why? Product and presentation. If you have the right product, customers will find you. If you have great presentation and a friendly staff, they will find you faster, buy more, and come back often.

How do the big guys keep their stores looking great all the time? Having a huge staff and an even bigger budget certainly helps, but there are techniques that you can adapt to your store for little or no cost that will help your store look better and sell more product.

SET STANDARDS

Have you noticed that at the Crate & Barrel all the handles point to the right? At Restoration Hardware everything is straight and square on the shelves, never angled? Bed, Bath, and Beyond stacks their merchandise up to the ceiling, far out of a customer's reach, for visual effect. These are examples of display standards, set by the visual merchandising teams in those chains. Look at your store and envision how it should look. Do you want your shelves stocked full all the time or do you prefer the merchandise arranged sparingly? In the original boxes or out of them? All price stickers should be in the same position on products. Do you want the tags on the tops or bottom? Left or right?

Write these things down. Tell your employees. All these little, almost invisible details will add up to a better-looking store.

While you are at it, how do you want your staff to answer the phone? Tell them how you'd like it done!

GREET YOUR CUSTOMERS

Customers should always feel welcome in your store. Your staff should be readily available, say hello, and offer suggestions; but they should not be breathing down the customer's necks unless they suspect shoplifting. Let's talk about greeters.

Consider the greeters at the mega-stores. They say hello and offer me a shopping cart, a useful and friendly service. Of course, I realize that the greeter at

TAG

"A person should not have to pay more for a well designed item than an ugly one. TAG's philosophy is to offer great products that are well designed and affordable. It takes a little more effort to design that product, but it doesn't cost much more to produce it.

"Also, you must change with the times and the needs of your customers."

Norman Glassberg
President
TAG

Wanamaker's

John Wanamaker, the founder of Wanamaker's in Philadelphia, was one of the pioneers of department store marketing. He is the man who first marked product with prices that end in 99 cents, which forced the clerks to ring up the sale and open the drawer to make change. This was a technique to avoid employee theft, not to make the price appear lower.

"Many persons have an idea that one cannot be in business and lead an upright life, whereas the truth is that no one succeeds in business to any great extent, who misleads or misrepresents"

—John Wanamaker

Best Buy is really a security guy on the lookout for theft, so I understand why he is waiting at the door. However, I am sometimes irritated when greeted by a person planted at the door of a specialty store, saying hello and offering help before I am even all the way in the store. These greeters often cannot leave their posts if someone needs help, although they can point you to another salesperson for the desired product. Additionally, they often look bored because saying "Hello! Welcome to our store" one hundred and eleven times an hour gets old pretty fast.

Teach your staff to be available and helpful, but not to attack customers as they arrive. Salespeople should assist the customers, not accost them.

SHOPPING BASKETS

Give your customers a helping hand! Have baskets available in several places in the store, and instruct your staff to offer them to the buyers. If a customer has a full basket, give her a new one and offer to keep the first one at the counter. People often think they are finished shopping when their hands are full—so give them the assistance they need to keep shopping.

NAME TAGS

Give your staff name tags. Name tags are almost like introductions—your customers will often address your staff by name. If you run any type of sales incentive or commission program that requires the cashier to track sales, name tags are imperative. Don't put your customers in the position of having to describe your staff! I recently watched a customer trying hard to describe a sales associate without using the word fat. When your staff grows at the holidays, name tags help them learn each other's names as well.

Take a few tips from the big stores to give your store the polish it deserves.

47

My Christmas at the Crate & Barrel

"Christmas is for kids" is a popular and sweet sentiment. In my family, we have always felt that it should be "Christmas is for retail." Fourth quarter is the make-it-or-break-it time for most gift stores, with some stores reporting as much as 60% of their volume from seasonal sales. Having grown up in retail, wrapping gifts and working long hours in December is as much a part of the holiday experience as school pageants and fruitcake. For the first 13 years of my marriage, my husband was absent for the month of December, chained to the register at his store. On Christmas day, after Mass, presents, and breakfast, my husband would head into his shop to stage the merchandise for the after-Christmas sale. My husband, the kids, and I all worked at his store during the final season at that location, closing the store on December 31, 2001.

Christmas 2002 was unnatural in our household. There was no store. We were home for all the parties. The kids had real dinners every night, with the whole family at the table. We had time for Christmas cards and cookies, special holiday outings, and family togetherness. We even went shopping with the crowds on the day after Thanksgiving and bargain hunted on December 26.

It just wasn't us. We missed the mad scramble to get to the store on time. We longed for the stories of wild crowds, nutty customers, and desperate last-minute purchases. We missed telling total strangers what to buy for family and friends we had never met. Our children felt hemmed in and over-parented. The local pizza shop reported declining sales without our frequent orders. We had nothing to do the day after Christmas, and felt a terrible post holiday let down.

The next Christmas we returned to normal. Partly for fun and partly for research (and, in my case, for the shopping), my husband and I took holiday jobs. It was fascinating and incredibly educational to work for national chain stores after our many years of experience in independent retail. I interviewed at several mall stores and compared their packages for part-time, seasonal help. All the stores at which I applied needed big holiday staffs, and every one offered me a job. These stores really market to their potential employees, offering three major incentives: discounts of 30% to 40%, flexible hours, and fun. While they pay well by retail standards, usually $8.00 per hour in this market, it is not the monetary compensation that attracts most of their seasonal help. It is the experience and the discount.

I chose Crate & Barrel and had a wonderful two-month career there until the real world pulled me back. By the way, it was a very profitable job. I think I made several dollars more than I spent, although that has not been verified. I did spend far more than any other seasonal employee, I was cheerfully told.

Working at the Crate felt more like working for an independent store owner than a large company (a really big, successful, organized, well-run, independent store). The managers frequently mentioned the founder, Gordon Segal, by name. "Gordon doesn't like that." "Gordon says we can put these boxes on the floor." "Gordon is coming to town." While I met Gordon only on a video, he was a very real presence in the store, and I always felt that he might just drop in. It impressed me to see how important the owner-operator feeling is to the staff and customers.

"Keep up the old standards, and day by day raise them higher"

—John Wanamaker

What's the big deal about the Crate? First, they have great merchandise. The store has a good selection, and it is almost always in stock. In addition, there is invariably some fun seasonal product that changes frequently. The shoppers know that they will find what they need and can look forward to some surprises.

What is the core product of your store? What do shoppers depend on you to carry? Defining that merchandise and keeping it in stock are huge steps towards positioning your store for success.

Pricing is very important. Almost every day I heard a shopper compare the Crate's prices to other stores in the mall, always favorably. When consumers feel that your prices are fair on the little stuff, they are more comfortable spending money on expensive merchandise because they trust you. Set your retails carefully! While you want the highest margins you can get, you must keep retail prices in line with your competition.

Customers don't wait to buy until there is a sale. While there are always a few mark-downs in the store, the Crate has only one big sale a year, right after Christmas. This is a huge event, with product brought in just for the sale, but it doesn't impact their regular business. Their customers know they have to buy the product when they see it during the season, because most merchandise never goes on sale.

Whether your marketing plan calls for one sale annually or several smaller events, create excitement with your clearance. Promote it, talk about it ahead of time to every customer, and invite every customer to come back for the bargains. Have firm beginning and end dates, and always shop for off-price merchandise that you can sell at sale prices while still achieving a full mark-up.

Crate & Barrel stores always look fresh, exciting, and full. While they have exacting standards and a clear display philosophy, the individual store merchandisers adapt the displays to suit their stores. When a display starts to look a little tired, before it becomes picked over, they change it. And the stores are clean. They use a lot of glass cleaner at the Crate, I can tell you from first-hand experience.

Keeping the store looking great must be a priority for every shop, regardless of size or budget. Every time you move the merchandise in your store around, it looks new to the shoppers. Sometimes it is just a matter of finding the right spot for product to start selling.

Part of the secret to a pleasant shopping experience is happy help. The Crate's salespeople are well trained and familiar with the merchandise. While you may not be able to offer the benefits only a large company can afford, letting your staff know how important they are and doing everything you can to make their jobs rewarding pay off at the cash register. One of the conveniences most appreciated by the staff is flexible scheduling, by the way.

Crate & Barrel is a Mom and Pop operation brought to its highest level. They treat their employees as much like family as anybody with 6,000 family members can. Their website says it very clearly: they focus on the three P's—People, Product, and Presentation.

Every store should do the same.

"If you work just for money, you'll never make it, but if you love what you're doing and you always put the customer first, success will be yours."

—Ray Kroc
Founder
McDonald's

Source Pages

PRODUCTS

Somerset Entertainment ....www.somersetent.com
TerraNova Bath and Body ....www.terranovabody.com
The Paper Company.. www.thepaperco.com
The Thymes, Ltd... www.thymes.com
Three Designing Women ....www.threedesigningwomen.com
Tipperary Crystal ....www.tipperarycrystal.com
Two's Company...www.twoscompany.com
Waterford Crystal ....www.waterford.com

TRADE SHOW

Americasmart ....www.americasmart.com
Columbus Gift Mart....................................www.thecolumbusmarketplace.com
Craft and Hobby Association (CHA) ....www.hobby.org
Dallas Market Center ....www.dallasmarketcenter.com
Denver Gift Mart .... www.denvermart.com
Enterprise Ireland...www.enterprise-ireland.com
George Little Management .... www.glmshows.com
    Handbook (exhibitors) ....www.glmshows.com/press/display.htm
    Handbook (retailers) ....www.glmshows.com/press/DisplayHandbook
Kansas City Gift Mart...kcgiftmart.com
Minneapolis Gift Mart ....www.mplsgiftmart.com
National Home Furnishing Association .... www.nhfa.org
Northeast Market Center .... www.thegiftcenter.com
Urban Exhibitions ....www.urban-expo.com
Western Exhibitors ....www.weshows.com
Western Home Furnishing Association...www.whfa.org

MISCELLANEOUS

amFAR.. www.amfar.com
Andrew J. Pinard Publication Consulting.................... www.andrewjpinard.com
Richard Bains .... www.lasikvisionwindsor.com
eBay .... www.ebay.com
Eller Enterprises ....www.ellerent.com
Gift for Life ....www.giftforlife.org
Leon & Lulu..www.leonandlulu.com
Mary Liz Curtin & Company ....www.marylizcurtin.com
Overcoffee Productions .... www.overcoffee.com

STORE WRAP SOURCES

Gift Box Corporation of America www.800giftbox.com

Howard Decorative Packaging .... www.hdponline.com
Hupaco, The Hudson Paper Company .... www.hudsonpaper.com
Nashville Wraps .... www.nashvillewraps.com
S. Walter Packaging .... www.swalter.com
Sample House .... www.samplehouse.com
U.S.Box .... www.usbox.com

ASSOCIATIONS AND GROUPS

Accessory Resource Team .... www.accessoriesresourceteam.org
American Booksellers Association .... www.bookweb.org
American Specialty Toy
    Retailing Association (ASTRA) .... www.astratoy.org
Awards and Recognition Association .... www.ara.org
California State Floral Association .... www.calstatefloral.com
Craft and Hobby Association (CHA) .... www.hobby.org
Export Promotion Council
    for Handicrafts of India (EPCH) .... www.epch.com
Gift Association of America .... www.giftassoc.org
Greeting Card Association .... www.greetingcard.org
It's Another .... www.itsanother.org
Michigan Retailers Association .... www.retailers.com
Museum Store Assciation .... www.museumdistrict.com
National Association
    of Limited Edition Dealers .... www.naled.com
National Association
    of Visual Merchandisers .... www.visualmerch.com
National Retail Federation .... www.nrf.com
National Retail Hardware Association .... www.nhra.org
North American Celtic Buyers Association .... www.celticbuyers.com
Party Club of America .... www.partyclubofamerica.com
Purchasing Power Plus .... www.purchasingpowerplus.com
Retail Advantage Group .... www.retailadvantagegroup.com
Retail Confectioners Association
    of Philadelphia, Inc .... www.phillycandyshow.com
Shop.org .... www.shop.org
Society of American Florists .... www.safnow.org

BUSINESS PLAN WEBSITES

Planware .... www.planware.org/bizplan.htm
Entrepreneur magazine .... www.entrepreneur.com/bizplan

Inc. magazine ....www.inc.com/guides/write_biz_plan
Small Business Administration
        ....www.sba.gov/starting_business/planning/basic.html
Bplans.com .... www.bplans.com/sp/businessplans.cfm

PHONE COMPARISON SITES

Hometown Phone .... www.hometownphone.com
Saveonphone.com .... www.saveonphone.com

Worksheet

Copy this worksheet as often as you would like and use it with the chapters you find particularly important for your store.

What were the key points for your store in this chapter?

Give yourself credit: What do you do now that works well?

To Do Now List

1.

2.

3.

To-Do Later List

1.

2.

3.

New Idea or Inspiration?

About Mary Liz Curtin

Mary Liz Curtin is passionate about independent retail. She grew up in retail, married a store owner and now she and her husband own a furniture, gift and accessory store called Leon & Lulu in Clawson, Michigan.

Mary Liz is a popular speaker at trade shows, conventions and industry conferences, addressing shopkeepers, manufacturers and sales professionals in the gift, home and craft industries. Her column, The Penny Pinching Retailer appears monthly inside the back cover of Giftware News magazine. She also writes frequently for greetings, etc. and Floral Management magazines, among others.

Mary Liz has worked in all aspects of the industry starting her career as an independent sales representative, and then managing sales and marketing at the national level, becoming Dominatrix of Sales for Fante Stationery and then Empress of Sales for Mrs. Grossman's Paper Company.

In 1993 Mary Liz used her extensive field knowledge to begin her consulting career. She has worked with established companies, emerging manufacturers, sales representatives and retailers, advising on marketing, sales and management issues. She is a member of the National Speaker's Association, sits on the board of Paper House Productions, Inc. and is a retail consultant to eBay.

She chairs the board of Gift for Life, the industry volunteer charity organization that raises money for AIDS research and education through the auspices of amfAR, the American Foundation for Aids Research.

Mary Liz lives in Michigan with her patient and understanding husband, their two generally well-behaved children, one exceedingly large lap dog and three cats. By the way, the store is named for Lulu, the rottweiler lap dog, and Leon, their 15 year old alpha cat.